Welcome to the *EVERYTHING*® series!

These handy, accessible books give you all you need to tackle a difficult project, gain a new hobby, comprehend a fascinating topic, prepare for an exam, or even brush up on something you learned back in school but have since forgotten.

You can read an *EVERYTHING*® book from cover to cover or just pick out the information you want from our four useful boxes: e-facts, e-ssentials, e-alerts, and e-questions. We literally give you everything you need to know on the subject, but throw in a lot of fun stuff along the way, too.

We now have well over 100 *EVERYTHING*® books in print, spanning such wide-ranging topics as weddings, pregnancy, wine, learning guitar, one-pot cooking, managing people, and so much more. When you're done reading them all, you can finally say you know *EVERYTHING*®!

FACTS

Important sound bytes
of information

SSENTIALS

Quick handy tips

ALERT

Urgent warnings

QUESTIONS?

Solutions to
common problems

Dear Reader,

Growing up in rural Minnesota has given me a special appreciation for the independent businessperson. As a child, I saw these people not as the purveyors of products, but as vital links to the bigger world. The Watkins man brought delicious spices we couldn't get in our small-town grocery store. The Avon lady brought equally exotic perfumes. We got our hard-to-find grooming items from the Fuller Brush man and shiny plastic containers from the Tupperware lady.

These people also played an important role in our lives because they were our friends and neighbors. We bought their products because we trusted these people. We looked forward to their visits as a chance to see what was new in the world and to catch up on neighborhood news. Our lives were intertwined with these salespeople and, not surprisingly, became equally intertwined with their products.

So it comes as no surprise that most of my family and friends have tried their hands at network marketing. Whether it was a fleeting interest or a lifelong pursuit, we realized the satisfaction it could bring as we did what came naturally—bringing a part of the larger world to our friends.

Margaret Kaeter

THE
EVERYTHING®
NETWORK
MARKETING
BOOK

How anyone can achieve easy success,
earn a great income, and enjoy a
relaxing lifestyle

Margaret Kaeter

Adams Media Corporation
Avon, Massachusetts

EDITORIAL
Publishing Director: Gary M. Krebs
Managing Editor: Kate McBride
Copy Chief: Laura MacLaughlin
Acquisitions Editor: Eric Hall
Development Editor: Julie Gutin
Production Editor: Khrysti Nazzaro

PRODUCTION
Production Director: Susan Beale
Production Manager: Michelle Roy Kelly
Series Designer: Daria Perreault
Cover Design: Paul Beatrice and Frank Rivera
Layout and Graphics: Colleen Cunningham,
Rachael Eiben, Michelle Roy Kelly, Daria Perreault

An Everything® Series Book.
Everything® is a registered trademark of Adams Media Corporation.

Published by Adams Media Corporation
57 Littlefield Street, Avon, MA 02322 U.S.A.
www.adamsmedia.com

ISBN: 1-58062-736-6
Printed in the United States of America.

J I H G F E D C B A

Library of Congress Cataloging-in-Publication Data
Kaeter, Margaret.
The everything network marketing book / Margaret Kaeter.
p.   cm.   —(An everything series book)
Includes index.
ISBN 1-58062-736-6
1. Multilevel marketing. I. Title. II. Series: Everything series.
HF5415.126 .K348 2003
2002014336

This publication is designed to provide accurate and authoritative information with regard to the subject matter covered. It is sold with the understanding that the publisher is not engaged in rendering legal, accounting, or other professional advice. If legal advice or other expert assistance is required, the services of a competent professional person should be sought.
—From a *Declaration of Principles* jointly adopted by a Committee of the American Bar Association and a Committee of Publishers and Associations

Illustrations by Barry Littmann.

This book is available at quantity discounts for bulk purchases.
For information, call 1-800-872-5627.

Visit the entire Everything® series at everything.com

Dedication

To my father, Jim Kaeter, who knew that I should work for myself long before I would admit it.

Acknowledgments

To Ruth Petermann, Tom Kaeter, Kathleen Rustad, Julie Tilka, and all my cousins and friends who have been network marketers, for their insight; to my husband, Michael Olesen, for his business and management advice; to my daughters, Gretchen and Emma Olesen, for their encouragement; to Dick Schaaf and all those business magazine editors whose assignments gave me the knowledge to write this book; and to Eric Hall, a very patient editor who has his priorities firmly in place.

Contents

Introduction

Network marketing has had a place in the world of business since the early days of commerce. From the day a craftsman discovered that he could make more money if he asked friends and family to take his products to neighboring towns and sell them in exchange for a small part of the proceeds, businesspeople have known that it makes sense to branch out and build a sales network that works for you.

In this age of international business and multibillion-dollar corporations, many people have forgotten that nothing happens in business until one person buys something from another person. All those sophisticated technologies and distribution systems are worthless unless the product is actually sold.

As the world becomes more fast-paced and complex, we seem to need to go back to our personal relationships. We are gravitating back to our families and friends for support in an uncertain, too-hectic world. Business trends also show that consumers are doing business with smaller and smaller companies every day. They want the personal contact. They want to know the person they are doing business with. They want to talk about their kids as they peruse the latest catalog of products. They appreciate your taking the time to find the best items for them.

In fact, owning a network-marketing business is no different from running any small business. What makes network marketing such an exciting venture is that you are always working for yourself. You get out of it what you put into it. And yes, if you put your mind to it, you can make millions.

People like to point out that you make money in network marketing through the hard work of other people. That's true. You get a percentage of the sale from every person you have personally helped start up in business. In return, however, you are coaching these people, giving them the creative ideas and expertise you have gleaned from working the business day in and day out.

Does that sound familiar? It should, because it's exactly how every company in the world operates. Doesn't the top executive of a company ultimately make her money from the hard work of the frontline salesperson? Of course she does. In the same way, you can make money from the people who work for you.

This process of building up your team—your down-line—is what separates network marketing from other small business opportunities. Nowhere else do you get to run your own business your way while the people who work for you also get to run their own businesses using their own ideas and styles. You encourage and coach them, but you aren't technically their boss. They come to you for advice and ideas, but you can't tell them exactly what to do because you all are independent business owners.

Your down-line is just a small part of the network you will use when you get into network marketing. Think of a spider and the complex network of threads it uses to build a web to catch its meals. Our world is a lot like that of a spider. In fact, sometimes some of us are spinning so fast in so many directions that we may forget the reason we're building a web at all!

However, if you sit back and examine that web closely, you'll see that it is a fine network made up of many different groups of people—your family, neighbors, friends, acquaintances, and even your church. This is the real network in network marketing, because these are the people you will go to as you build your business.

Much of the information in this book is simply good common sense about starting and running an at-home business. Network marketing isn't for everybody, but this book will help you decide if it's right for you, and it will help get you started once you have made the decision.

CHAPTER 1

Make Your Fortune with Network Marketing

Network marketing is a proven, highly successful way of making money. Many people have become wealthy running network-marketing businesses because it is one of the few business methods that lets an individual run their business in the way that is right for them and their customers, yet also offers the full support of a larger organization.

Some Definitions Are in Order

First off, let's define "marketing." Marketing is the way businesses tell consumers about their products. There is no great magic or mystery to making marketing work. It is simply a matter of figuring out how best to convince a group of people that they need to give something a try. Television ads, newspaper ads, billboards, direct-mail pieces, and phone solicitations are all forms of marketing that you experience virtually every day. You may even take them for granted, as a basic part of your life.

Marketing Is Good

Can you imagine life without any advertisements or salespeople? It wouldn't be as easy as you might first think. How would you know when a new product is on the market? How would you know that a company improved one of its old products? How would you know that there is a product that can ease your pain or solve a major problem in your life?

Getting that information wouldn't be easy. It would take a great deal of time and energy to find the items you needed. Your life would be harder because you wouldn't know about things that could make it easier. Your life would also be a lot less fun because you would spend most of it searching for the basic items you need to live, such as food and clothing.

**SSENTIALS**

In a sense, marketing is a service profession. Although there is no question that some people may take it well beyond the ethical boundaries of service and into manipulation or even coercion, good marketing is simply about helping people.

Adding "Network" to Marketing

Network marketing is simply a type of marketing, a way to tell people about a product they might need. However, instead of using advertisements, network marketing relies on distributors. According to the U.S. Federal Trade Commission, that is the only thing that distinguishes it from other forms of marketing and sales.

Some companies sell their products through retail outlets, others send out direct-mail catalogs; some take advantage of the World Wide Web, and others rely on professional salespeople. Network marketing companies use distributors who usually work part-time to relay a particular company's message about its products directly to the customers.

What Sets Network Marketing Apart

Selling products through distributors may seem a simple explanation of the difference between network marketing and other types of marketing. However, those four words are very crucial. Let's look at them individually:

- Network marketing involves selling, not just communicating the benefits of a product.
- Network marketing involves real products. It can't be an "investment opportunity" that relies on the recruitment of other people to make your money.
- Even the word *through* is critical. The company doesn't sell *to* distributors—it sells *through* them. Eventually, people who are not distributors for the company should be using at least a portion of the items sold by the company.
- Network marketing must involve distributors—people who sell to many other people. Distributors don't sell just to themselves and they don't just hire other distributors.

Legitimate network-marketing programs involve selling a tangible product. If you are selling something you can't touch or see, or if your sponsor tells you there is no selling involved, investigate further to ensure it is a legitimate enterprise.

Multilevel Marketing

The distributor portion of network marketing is the reason many people call it multilevel marketing. You are building a distribution business that brings product from a central location to distributors and finally to an individual. There may be several levels, but eventually they all lead back to the same place—the company that makes the items.

The multiple levels are important because they determine how much money you receive from each sale. Usually, but not always, the closer you are to the top, the larger percentage of the sale you will receive.

Direct Selling

Sometimes network marketing is also called "direct sales" because you are selling product directly to the end user. Even if you are spending the majority of your time building a down-line of distributors, someone somewhere in your down-line is selling directly to an end user. That is what makes this a direct-selling opportunity.

Network Marketing Is Big Business

Network marketing is much more than a sales and marketing tool. It is an opportunity for virtually anyone to become a millionaire. The Direct Selling Association (DSA) estimates that network marketing is a $100-billion business worldwide. The association's research also shows that about 50,000 Americans a week begin working in network marketing at least part-time.

FACTS

According to the Direct Selling Association, approximately one in four Americans will give network marketing a try at some point in their lives. Most will quit after less than one year, but about 10 percent of those who try it will make a career of it.

Most people are familiar with the major names in network marketing: Shaklee, Tupperware, Avon, Fuller Brush, Mary Kay, Amway, and Watkins, to name just a few. These companies were founded on the network-marketing principle and have continued to thrive using this marketing method.

In addition, approximately 100 new network-marketing companies are established every year. Many of these will fail, but about ten of them will become long-term business endeavors that offer real opportunities for people to make good money.

It's Just That Easy

Network marketing is popular because it is easy and it gives you control over your life. What other jobs let you set your own hours and do exactly what you want to achieve your goals? Other small-business opportunities require you to put in specific hours or file special reports with other people in the business. In virtually every other type of opportunity that allows you to work at home, you are directly reporting to someone else who is in charge of making sure you get your work done.

With network marketing, you are in charge. You decide how hard you will work. You decide exactly what work you will do. And you decide how, when, and where you will get that work done.

QUESTIONS?

Do you love to talk to people?
Believe it or not, virtually everyone in the world likes to talk to other people. You might not like strangers, but you certainly like to talk to your friends, right? Guess what? In network marketing, you are actually working as you are talking to your friends.

There is nobody looking over your shoulder forcing you to work instead of going fishing on a beautiful summer morning. There is no one screaming if you don't make the quota or making you feel guilty for attending your son's school play instead of getting more work done.

Network marketing allows you to take control of your income. The harder—and smarter—you work, the more money you will make. If you just want a few extra dollars every month, network marketing can provide that. If you want to become a millionaire in ten years, network marketing can also provide that.

Network Marketing Works

More and more entrepreneurs are bringing their products to the marketplace using network marketing because it is an efficient and effective sales strategy. It involves less work, less money, and less time than any other new business strategy.

Network marketing relies on the age-old tradition of relationship building to make its sales. Instead of hiring professional salespeople who must work for months and years to gain the trust of their prospective customers, network marketing has built-in trust because new distributors automatically begin selling by working with people they already know.

Network marketing allows for more flexibility. While network-marketing companies certainly have to follow the laws and ethics of good business practice, keeping their operations smaller and with fewer full-time employees allows them more room and more options for moving into other business areas.

An Inexpensive Approach

Network marketing is a wonderful way for a new product to break into the marketplace, because it requires very little start-up cost. Imagine how much it costs a company to expand into a new area. It must rent office space, buy computers and other office equipment, and hire full-time salespeople. This venture is often too expensive, especially if the product has a low profit margin or a very small customer base.

Because network marketing relies on personal relationships to sell products, you don't even need high-quality sales brochures. In fact, some companies purposely rely on photocopies and other simple pieces of literature to tell their stories because the customers then know that their money isn't going to pay for expensive paper and printing.

A Practice Primed for Growth

Network marketing also is an excellent way to expand a business internationally. While major corporations continue to struggle with the problems of competing on an international level, network-marketing companies find that their only concern is finding reliable shipping organizations. Fortunately, customers are willing to pay the shipping costs, so that isn't a barrier to sales.

FACTS

Because network-marketing opportunities are easily expanded to international marketplaces, they are expected to be one of the fastest-growing small business types during the first half of the twenty-first century. A growing international population offers nearly limitless opportunities for selling product.

In this way, many network-marketing companies have found themselves quickly developing international markets and even competing with product lines they couldn't compete with in the United States. For example, when a line of natural health supplements that uses network marketing was able to break into the European market before any major pharmaceutical company came up with a competing product line, this company gained a loyal market share, thus thwarting other business's attempts to steal its customers.

Many Products to Choose From

Another reason network marketing is so popular is that it works well for selling many items. For example, you don't need a college degree or specialized training to help a customer pick out some beauty products. If you're selling a new line of detergents, you can probably explain what makes this line better than its competitors without a degree in chemistry. The same is true for most successful network-marketing opportunities.

Products that are perfect for network-marketing sales should have the following characteristics:

- Portability
- Competition in its general product category
- Truly unique features
- Sales potential to individuals, not groups
- Simplicity (it should be easy to demonstrate)
- Affordability

Why don't all companies use network marketing?
Network marketing is the right choice for items that are small and easily sold to individual people in small amounts. It would be impossible to sell large pieces of equipment through network marketing.

Network Marketing Goes Corporate

Toward the end of the twentieth century, intense business competition in select marketplaces collided with a rapid increase in online purchasing, and even big business caught on to the value this marketing method can deliver. Companies as diverse as CitiGroup, Dupont, MCI, Sprint, and Amazon.com began to use network marketing as a way to compete in this new world.

Both MCI and Sprint were able to successfully compete against the well-entrenched AT&T by offering their customers a small commission if a friend or family member signed up for the service. Fledgling Internet businesses such as Amazon.com and PayPal.com realized that offering online visitors a small payment for every friend who visits their site increased their customer base.

The Personal Touch

In the most basic sense, every company uses some type of network marketing to "get the word out" about its products. We just don't always recognize it. For example, every time a friend tells you to go to a new restaurant he tried last week, or to use a different floor-cleaning product because it works better, that company is taking advantage of an informal form of network marketing. Whether you like it or not, your personal relationship led to the sale of a product.

Some businesses even rely on this method of sales. For example, when a pharmaceutical company developed a product that would ease the specific pain of breast cancer for chemotherapy patients, it didn't bother advertising the product. Instead, it went to breast cancer support group leaders and relied on them to spread the word. The psychology of network marketing is one of its biggest advantages. People feel that you are doing them a favor, not trying to coerce them into something.

As companies look for ways to fight the mass-marketing strategies of major corporations, increasingly they will turn to down-home, personal marketing strategies that offer real help from real friends.

At the same time, as consumers are drowned by the many products and marketing messages, they will come to rely more on salespeople who can help them sort the good from the bad. They will turn to people they can trust and turn away from products that seem to be all hype.

A Few Common Misconceptions

Network marketing has gotten a bad reputation in the last fifty years or so, but this reputation is undeserved. True network marketing is ethical and honest. The company follows all the business laws and does not try to cheat either its distributors or the customers.

Unfortunately, it can be difficult to weed the good from the bad. Every year, there are dozens of unethical or dishonest companies entering the business of network marketing. They use this business strategy as nothing more than a way to dupe naive people and thus make a quick buck, and they prey on the people who are tired of working for large corporations and who want control over their lives and their incomes.

Luckily, the Federal Trade Commission as well as the attorneys general of all fifty states quickly discover these companies and put them out of business. It is a rare network-marketing company that is still in business two years after it has started unless it is honest and ethical.

No Vapor

A real network-marketing opportunity does not promote "vapor" products—items that are not what the company claims them to be. For example, several years ago a network-marketing company was selling a product that claimed to replace the need for laundry detergent. According to them, a little gizmo that looked like a donut-shaped piece of rubber could do the job of cleaning a load of wash. How did this work? Well, the reasons were "technical and complex," involving "advanced physics."

Do not accept "fuzzy" explanations for a product's performance. Your sponsor should be able to explain in real terms that you can understand how the item works and why it is different from competing products. Otherwise, you may be looking at a vapor product.

Although it sold very quickly and thousands of people signed up to become distributors, a national television show found that the product left your laundry as dirty as before it was washed—it was simply a donut-shaped piece of rubber filled with water.

Within days of that report, the product was nowhere to be seen and the thousands of people who had signed up as distributors lost their investment money along with their dreams of financial security and the trust of their customers.

Remember, if it sounds too good to be true, it probably is. A good network-marketing opportunity should contain no mysteries about the product, the work, or how you will get paid.

Beware the Pyramid

One reason network marketing has gotten its bad reputation is because of the proliferation of pyramid schemes. On the surface, pyramid schemes may look like network-marketing programs. However, they have one major difference: Pyramid schemes don't revolve around a viable product. They rely solely on recruiting distributors; new recruiters are only rewarded for finding other distributors. There may be a nominal product but no one is really encouraged to sell it.

Most states have passed laws against pyramid selling because they mislead the consumer. Think about it from a purely mathematical standpoint. If there is no item being purchased or if the product is a "last-a-lifetime" item, the distribution chain will eventually reach a saturation point. When everyone who could possibly be involved has become a distributor, there is nowhere else to go. The newest distributors become frustrated because they can't find new people to recruit. The older distributors stop making money because no one new is being recruited. Soon everyone is asking, "What happened to that miracle product?"

ALERT

Ask your potential sponsor what you should spend your first months doing. If he or she says you should begin recruiting new distributors, it may be a pyramid scheme. If he or she tells you to learn about the products, you know you have a legitimate company.

Ponzi No More

Ponzi schemes take pyramid schemes one step further. In a Ponzi scheme, there is no product at all and no bonuses for recruiting new members. What you get is a promise of a high return for "investing" your money. In fact, your investment is going to pay people higher up in the chain.

Like pyramid operations, Ponzi schemes are illegal in most states because they are a way to cheat people out of their money. People at the top do make a lot, but those who join in later on in the game inevitably lose hundreds and even thousands of dollars while they are waiting for their investment to "mature."

Be aware of possible pyramid or Ponzi schemes. Signals that should alert you include the following:

- Plans that offer a commission for recruiting distributors
- Plans that claim to sell miracle products (if it is too good to be true, more than likely it isn't a real product)
- Plans that ask new distributors to spend a great deal of money to buy inventory or to "buy into" the company
- Plans that talk only about making money through your down-line and ignore the sale of products
- Plans that are secretive about their name or their product attributes until after a presentation is made

- Plans that offer little or no product information for you or customers but do offer information on how to convince people to become distributors
- Plans that promise phenomenal earnings for no work

It's Time to Take It Seriously

As you look at all the factors discussed in this chapter, it quickly becomes clear that network marketing offers a very real opportunity for realizing your dreams. It can give you both personal and financial freedom because of its unique attributes.

It is a highly regarded, tried-and-true business marketing and sales strategy that is going to become more important in the future. As consumers look for ways to simplify their lives and smaller companies look for ways to compete with large international conglomerates, network marketing will take on a greater role in the business world.

FACTS

Perhaps one of the most important advantages of network marketing is its flexibility. This method offers you the chance to make money the way you want, and nearly any personality type can use it because it allows you to work the way you want. With a lot of perseverance and some creativity, network marketing can work in any area of the world.

In addition, thanks to better regulations and a greater awareness on the part of the consumer that network marketing is a valid and often beneficial way to buy product, this business technique is quickly losing the bad reputation it gained during the latter half of the twentieth century. The more good network-marketing companies we see in the marketplace, the more likely that unscrupulous people will turn to other methods for trying to cheat people.

CHAPTER 2
Some Business Basics

Network marketing is a distinct type of business. Just as running an airline is different from running a movie theater, there are aspects of network marketing that you won't find in any other type of business endeavor. This chapter will show you how the network-marketing business model compares to other types of business and will illustrate some basic approaches to network marketing.

Network Marketing and Conventional Business

Chances are good that your only working experience to date is in a conventional setting. You go into a building, whether it's an office, a factory, or a store, and you work several hours a day. You report to a supervisor or a manager. You may be paid an hourly wage or a yearly salary. Your company provides you with some benefits, like a retirement plan and health insurance.

Of course, there are some good things about this kind of work. As long as the company is doing well, you know you will have a steady paycheck. You can get promoted. You can gain experience that can be used at other jobs at other companies. You get little raises every year that usually keep up with the cost of living, so if you can feed your family today, you will likely be able to next year, too.

FACTS

According to a study by the University of Ohio, approximately 1,500 people start small or home-based businesses every day. About one-fourth of those new businesses are in network-marketing organizations and about three-fourths are people who want to work part-time.

But there is little you can really do to change your life. If you're very lucky, you may work at a job that allows you to work from home or lets you work part-time, choosing the hours you want. Maybe you have a job where you get to meet people out of the office or work in a setting you really enjoy. And you might just be lucky enough to work in a job that offers you a financial bonus now and then. Those opportunities can make working in a conventional business fairly tolerable.

Why Work for Someone Else?

But no matter how much you say you like your job, you still are working for someone else. You have to live by their rules and work within their guidelines. You work under their deadlines to reach their goals. You don't get to reap the benefits of your hard work. If you make a big sale, your company will get most of the profit. If you keep customers happy, your company will get the benefit of customer loyalty. You just keep getting that same salary or wage.

On the other hand, your steady paycheck does depend on the livelihood of your company. What if your company is sold to another company that decides to close your division? Your company could suddenly find itself in financial troubles and end up eliminating your position, or you could be unlucky enough to work for an unscrupulous company that squanders its employees' retirement monies and ends up going out of business completely.

The Advantages of a Down-Line and an Up-Line

Perhaps the biggest difference between conventional work and network marketing is the fact that after a few years of hard work to build a strong down-line, you can stop selling and still have a good income. The people you have recruited and trained take over the sales work and you reap the benefits of building a strong sales organization—a percentage of the sales from everyone you personally brought into the program as well as everyone your down-line recruits bring in.

At the same time, you will have a number of people who are willing to coach you. These people, all part of your "up-line," want you to succeed, because by succeeding, you make money for them as well as yourself. They will share ideas and strategies for building your business, and they will applaud your success. That means no jealous coworkers and no competition for promotions. No sucking up to the boss in hopes of getting favors down the road. Your sponsor and the rest of your up-line will do everything in their power to help you succeed and they will be happy when you do.

Starting Your Own Business

One option many people look at when they decide to work for themselves is to start their own conventional business. Perhaps you have always wanted to own a small retail shop or a restaurant. Maybe you have a skill—as a house painter or auto mechanic—that lends itself to starting your own business.

For many people, that is a good choice. They bring the variety of skills and talents necessary to make such an endeavor work. But for the majority, starting a business alone, with no company to support them, is a frightening and daunting task. After all, there is so much a new business owner must keep track of:

- Legal issues
- Accounting systems
- Insurance
- Advertising and marketing
- Customer service
- How to get new customers

You would need to contact an expert for every one of these activities. In many cases, such as with the lawyer and accountant, you would likely have to pay a large retainer fee to make sure the person is available to help you at any time.

Now add to these headaches the fact that you must do everything yourself in a conventional small business. To succeed, you will need to *be* the accountant, the customer service representative, the advertising manager, the worker, and any other position that your business may require.

ALERT

A strong network-marketing company can offer many resources for you to use. And unlike franchise owners, you will be free to pick and choose the resources that best meet your needs.

However, when you align yourself with a network-marketing company, many of these things are taken care of for you. It's likely that the company will supply advertising programs and sales brochures. You will need to talk to a lawyer, an accountant, and an insurance representative, but the company can tell you what questions to ask and how to find the best professional for your needs. In some cases, such as insurance, the company may have a preferred provider already signed up that offers special deals to their distributors.

Franchise Programs

Many people also look into franchise opportunities when they consider working for themselves, a logical step, especially if you are more comfortable with a traditional work setting. Franchises offer you a chance to run your own small operation, hiring the people you want and establishing basic work rules.

However, franchise opportunities frequently are almost as constricting as conventional work situations. By buying a franchise, you buy the right to sell a company's products. The company, in turn, provides a well-advertised brand name and some very strict guidelines on what you can do and where you can do it. For example, many fast-food franchises demand that you buy all your products from them, that you serve specific items on the menu, and that you use their brand of everything from grill cleaners to napkins.

What Franchisers Offer

Franchisers typically provide a great deal of assistance in everything from prepaid advertising to ready-made accounting systems. However, every piece of assistance provided by the franchiser usually comes with the caveat that you can use only that system. For example, if the franchiser provides advertising slicks for you to put in the local newspaper, you likely will not be allowed to develop your own creative advertising. If the franchiser has developed an accounting software program, you might have to use it and would not be allowed to modify it to meet your specific needs.

Franchises do have something to offer. First, you do get to run the business the way you want on a day-to-day basis. You can hire friends and family members. You can work eighty hours a week yourself instead of hiring someone else. You can even hire a manager and retire on the income the franchise brings in.

You also get the profits from the business, so the harder and smarter you work, the better you will do financially. The home corporation usually offers financial incentives such as bonuses and luxury vacations for its top franchisees and may also have some good retirement programs and benefits packages that you can take advantage of.

Franchise Shortcomings

Still, the conventional-business setting of most franchises is restricting. The people at the home office evaluate your work every year and decide if you are worthy to keep the franchise. If you don't follow their rules to the letter, you could be asked to give it up.

You will no doubt have a lot of restrictions on the equipment and supplies, advertising, and location of your business. As a result, many franchise opportunities offer only the illusion of working for yourself.

FACTS

Virtually all network-marketing opportunities are designed to be operated out of a home office, saving you a great deal of money in start-up expenses as compared to any other type of business opportunity, whether a franchise operation or a conventional business.

Worse, most franchise opportunities are very expensive. Some, such as fast-food franchises, can cost hundreds of thousands of dollars. Even simple opportunities, such as a carpet-cleaning business, can carry a hefty price tag of $50,000 in franchise, equipment, and start-up costs.

In addition to the cost of buying the franchise, which you would either pay up front or over time, these opportunities almost always include ongoing fees of some sort. Some may charge a monthly or yearly flat fee or a sliding fee based on your revenues or other factors for a set number of years. Others require you to pay royalties on your revenues as long as you stay in business. Many require you to pay a maintenance fee that covers items such as national advertising programs.

Affiliate Programs

In affiliate programs, you are encouraged to find people and "drive" them to the company. For each person you find, you will receive a flat fee. You may receive a bonus after you refer a certain number of people. Or you may receive payment based on the referred customer's purchases—you may not get paid at all if the person you refer does not buy anything. In an affiliate program, you never receive a percentage of any of the purchases your referral makes.

Affiliate programs are very common with new Internet sites. They will offer you a $5 coupon usable on their site, for example, when a friend of yours visits the site the first time and lists you as their referral. Consequently, it is to your advantage to get as many people as you can to visit that site.

Your friends, in turn, are encouraged to "drive" people to the site with the same offer. In some larger programs, you receive a smaller bonus for everyone your friend drives to the site and increasingly smaller bonuses for everyone your friend's friend brings in.

"Affiliate" Does Not Mean "Network"

People frequently confuse affiliate programs with network marketing because the company is building a network of new customers and prospects. Like in a network-marketing program, one person builds a group that spreads out geometrically.

Your network-marketing company may call the members of your down-line your "affiliates" because they are naturally connected to you. However, don't confuse this with affiliate programs, which offer only flat fees based on new recruits or referrals, not commissions based on sales.

However, the biggest difference is that in an affiliate program you don't receive a commission for any sales; you merely receive a small amount of money for every new name that arrives on the company's doorstep. In fact, many programs offer you a bonus only for "first-generation" names, the people who name you as their referral.

The limits to these programs are obvious. Eventually you will exhaust your contacts. The company may decide to disband the program when it receives enough names to keep its salespeople busy or when it reaches a "critical mass" of customers (when enough people know about them that they feel their product or company is "common knowledge" in the marketplace).

A Variation on Affiliate Programs

Another type of affiliate program involves recruiting people who buy a set amount of product from you. Usually these programs involve purchasing a great deal of inventory and cost several thousand dollars to "buy into." Your goal is to get rid of your inventory by getting other people to buy it from you when they become new affiliates.

Instead of receiving a commission on sales, you receive a bonus for every person you bring into the network. You may receive bonuses as people you have brought in recruit others, but you are never rewarded for any direct sales of product.

Unless it is very rigidly structured to ensure that product is actually sold, this variation can quickly become a pyramid program. As such, it is illegal in the United States and would quickly be disbanded by the Federal Trade Commission.

Understanding Residual Income

Residual income is the small amount of money you earn off someone else's sale. The best way to explain it is to make a diagram:

1. Take out a pencil and paper and draw a little circle at the top: that's you. Let's say you make $100 a month off your network-marketing opportunity. Put $100 inside your circle.
2. Now put two circles directly beneath your circle. Those are two people you sponsor. Let's say you get $50 a month from each of

their sales. Now you are getting $200 a month and the only extra work you have is to motivate your new recruits.

3. Now let's say your two first-generation recruits each sponsor two people (that's four more circles) and you get $25 a month from each of those people's sales. Now you are getting $300 a month.

4. Now each of those people sponsor two people and you get $10 a month from those eight new people. Now you make $380 a month.

All of the money you make off your recruits' sales is called residual income because you don't make it yourself directly. You receive a residual because you were smart enough to bring these people into the business!

Geometric Growth

As you see from this simplified example, the money you make off someone else's sale decreases with the distance between you and the seller. (That isn't always the case, but we'll discuss it more in Chapter 7.) As a result, you want to sponsor as many people as possible (that is, have as many first-generation sellers as you can).

Still, the opportunities for making big money are good even if you have just a couple of people in your first generation. If your recruits are successful in recruiting other people, your network will experience geometric growth.

Your Network

"Network" is the term used to describe the geometric growth phenomenon. Instead of a direct line from you to someone below you, as in a traditional workplace, your network continues to branch out as people below you recruit new distributors.

The term "network" refers to other groups of people as well. For example, unless you started this company, you have a sponsor and your sponsor likely has a sponsor. All of those people, called your "up-line," are part of your network. You can call on any of them at any time to help you with your business.

Likewise, your direct customers belong to your network as well. Although it makes sense to spend most of your energy recruiting new distributors, there invariably will be relatives, friends, and even new acquaintances who aren't quite ready to take that step yet. They will continue to buy your products and, in turn, recommend those items to their friends; soon, you will have a network of people who are buying from you, too.

FACTS

In some situations (discussed in Chapter 7), the network forms a very prescribed shape. New recruits are placed into specific slots on an organizational chart. However, in most network-marketing opportunities today, you are free to recruit as many people as you can.

Internal-Consumption Programs

Internal-consumption programs don't encourage participants to sell products to others—the products are for the participants' own consumption only. These programs work because they manage to take advantage of "economies of scale"—the fact that a company can buy products more cheaply in bulk than you can find them at a retail store. You buy just what you need every month, as do all your down-line members, and you get a portion of the proceeds from your down-line's purchases.

However, these programs deserve a great deal of scrutiny because they can easily become illegal pyramid schemes where no product is really being sold. You will likely have the most difficult time getting people to join your down-line with these programs because you have no unique item to be enthusiastic about; the company may have what it calls "private label" products, but these are simply name-brand products that the company has purchased and labeled with its own name.

Amway sometimes works like an internal-consumption program because the vast majority of its items are available in retail markets. They offer their members a good price on these products, but the members, as a rule, are not encouraged to sell these items to individual consumers.

Instead, they are encouraged to sell the program to people who will buy the items for their own use.

To sell this type of program to a new recruit, you need to be able to explain the economics of the situation. In many cases, this is where these programs fail. People you are trying to recruit simply don't see how buying products for their own use can make them personally wealthy.

Marketing-Driven Programs

These programs rely on marketing programs that come from the home office to boost sales. People like the company's products for many reasons, but one of the most important is that there is always something on sale.

Frequently, marketing-driven programs are sensitive to the fluctuations in price. If the product's cost rises too much, customer loyalty will wane. They also tend to have the most competitors in the retail sector. Consequently, the sales can be unpredictable and erratic.

 **SSENTIALS**

Marketing-driven companies are probably the most fun to work for because there is always something new to sell. You can usually find a few direct sales every month because the items on sale are discounted so steeply that somebody will give them a try.

If You Like to Sell

Marketing-driven programs are wonderful for people who plan to continue direct selling as they build their down-line. They are great if you like to meet people and chat with your customers, because they give you an excuse to stop by every few weeks.

The only negative of a marketing-driven program is that you can become so focused on selling what's on sale that you forget to work on building your down-line.

Not surprisingly, few network-marketing opportunities are truly driven by marketing, while a good number of single-level direct-sales opportunities, such as Avon, are completely marketing-driven.

Name-Driven Programs

Name-driven programs are actually a subset of marketing-driven programs, but they deserve special attention because the strategy is very different. In these programs, such as Discovery Toys and Pampered Chef, the company markets the product line as a whole. There may be an occasional sale on an item, but the message to consumers is, "Anything you buy will be wonderful because it's part of our line."

Many new network-marketing companies attempt this form of marketing because they don't have a product reputation yet. They begin to build excitement over all the different things they offer so that customers want to see what everyone is talking about.

These programs have big income potential if you can get into the company's distribution system early—they frequently take off within a couple of years. The danger, however, is that the product line becomes "old news." Once customers have purchased once or twice, they have no reason to purchase again unless new items are added. The excitement of the initial communications may be impossible to regain if even one item doesn't live up to the blanket claim.

Product-Driven Programs

Product-driven programs rely on the strength of the product to sell as well as to build a down-line. They may be supported by marketing, such as brochures and an occasional sale, but they aren't marketing-driven because people don't buy the vast proportion of the items as a result of the steep discount.

Watkins would be a good example of a product-driven company. The product has had a strong name for more than 100 years and many of its customers are extremely loyal to the product. (The company was founded in the late 1800s on a small product line of food items, cleaning supplies, and personal care products. It continues to expand in those product lines.)

Watkins puts out monthly sales brochures that offer items for a small percentage less than the regular price—but don't mistake these for steep discounts. The purpose here is to highlight specific items every month and perhaps entice people who are thinking about buying the item to finally give it a try.

Customer Loyalty Drives Sales

Product-driven programs are strong because the customer loyalty is huge, and there is always a threat that the product's performance will falter, whether it's in reality or in the customer's mind. For example, if research comes out that caffeine is bad for elderly people and the company's popular multivitamin contains caffeine, the company might see a significant loss of sales.

Because of this, these programs require the company to conduct continuous research of the marketplace. For example, Watkins used to carry its Red Barn Salve in large containers, but the company found that customers weren't buying it as much anymore. Watkins switched to smaller containers that could be carried in a purse or stored in a small bathroom drawer, and the sales picked up again.

SSENTIALS

It's easy to build a down-line with a product-driven company because people like the items so much, they are willing to personally recommend them to their friends and family.

Putting It Together

It's no surprise that many network-marketing opportunities don't fit neatly into one of these categories. Many companies will experiment with different marketing styles as well as different compensation plans. Some will even bring in elements of conventional businesses and franchise programs.

The key is to remember that every aspect of the program is put in place for a reason. A solid company will know those reasons and be able to tell you what it hopes to achieve by using the strategy it has chosen.

CHAPTER 3

Is Network Marketing Right for You?

You have probably heard someone say they know a "natural" salesperson. "That guy could sell ice to the Eskimos and sand to the Arabs," they say. The fact is, all kinds of people can be successful in sales and network marketing. What it really takes is a desire to succeed and a willingness to talk to people.

It's Like Running a Business

Running a network-marketing business has many things in common with any form of self-employment—you must rely on yourself for much of the work. You are the receptionist, the secretary, the worker, the delivery person, and, of course, the leader. You must be able to change these hats at a moment's notice and you must be at least moderately capable in each of these roles.

Another factor common in all small businesses is that you must learn how to rely on other people. You can't afford to spend too much money on a lawyer or accountant, for example, so you have to know when you absolutely need this expertise and when you don't.

ESSENTIALS

Running a small business is a constant juggling act. If you're not careful you can spend your days working hard only to discover that you aren't getting anything important done. Or you can spend your days making sales only to find that the routine paperwork isn't getting done.

A Unique Undertaking

However, network marketing does differ from other types of self-employment. For example, while you work out of your home, you also have a large organization behind you. The company you will work with provides basic business materials such as advertising, sales brochures, and order forms. People in your up-line as well as at the home office are available to guide you through everything from setting up a Web site to teaching you basic selling skills.

You also have more flexibility than most self-employed people. You don't have to work from 8 A.M. to 5 P.M. because most of your customers are easy to reach in the evenings and on weekends. You can combine business with social visits. And eventually, when your down-line becomes large enough, you can even stop working altogether.

Personality Traits That Make It Work

Network marketing is a wonderful opportunity for many, many people. However, it isn't right for everyone. Some people are better off working for others. They need the consistency and security that comes from having someone else tell them what to do.

If you like a regular paycheck, knowing what your day is going to be like when you wake up, and having regular work hours, network marketing might not be a good fit for you. However, whether you see yourself as shy or outgoing, sophisticated or common, if you have the drive and desire to work for yourself, you can succeed in network marketing. You need just a few key personality traits to ensure your success.

Perseverance

A good network marketer never gives up. He or she understands that there are good times and bad times in every business and recognizes the importance of working through the bad times.

Ask yourself what you have done in your personal and work life when times got tough? Did you quit your job when the boss started asking too much from you? Did you divorce your spouse when you started having fights every night? Did you throw your hands in the air and give up when your teenagers caused problems? If that's the case, you might not have the perseverance it takes to make it in network marketing.

FACTS

People with perseverance are inherently optimistic. Their motto is, "Bad times never last." They know that world and local events can change a marketplace overnight. They realize that sometimes you need to just push through a problem and move on.

Passion

Network marketing takes a great deal of enthusiasm because you constantly have to overcome people's natural objections to buying from a "door-to-door salesperson." When you're trying to motivate someone to join your down-line, it can take even more passion, because you are asking someone to make a major lifestyle change. As any professional salesperson can tell you, the most important secret to selling is to truly believe in your product.

Ask yourself how you really feel about this venture. Do you want to "give it a try" or are you convinced that it's the best thing for you to do? Do you think the products you will be selling are the best on the market or are they fine products that aren't any better than others out there? Do you feel that being a distributor is a phenomenally fun and exciting way to make a living or do you see it as the only route you could take to make a million dollars?

Passionate people tend to burn hot and turn to cinders rather quickly. Learn to control your passion and save it for important times, such as recruitment meetings and other sales situations.

The answers to these questions determine your enthusiasm and passion. Yes, you want to make money doing this, but network marketing should be something you are so excited about that you can't imagine doing anything else. Ask yourself what you would do for a living if you really didn't need the money. If you would get out there, meet people, and convince them to buy something, you likely have the level of passion you need to make it in network marketing.

Outgoing Nature

There's no question about it. If you want to succeed in network marketing, you have to be able to get out there and meet people. Nothing happens in this business until someone buys something from another individual, and that won't happen if you stay home all day.

If you truly like working by yourself—analyzing numbers, inputting data, or sketching, for example—you probably wouldn't like network marketing. If you find people annoying and a hindrance to getting your real work done, you should probably look for other opportunities.

On the other hand, outgoing does not mean you have to be the life of the party. People who are outgoing like other people. They like to learn about other people and get into conversations with them about almost anything. They are fascinated by the differences in people and accept individuals at face value. They don't judge other people.

In fact, you likely don't want to be the life of the party. Think about it. Would you really buy something from someone who talks only about himself or herself and likes to be the center of attention?

You are outgoing if the following points apply to you:

- You find that when you are depressed you want to be with people.
- You are so energized when you meet a new person that you find it hard to sleep.
- You are a natural matchmaker, getting two or more people together with common interests.
- You look forward to meeting new people.
- You don't necessarily like big parties because you know that you won't be able to get into a long conversation with someone.
- You like to laugh at yourself.

Listening Skills

Whether you are selling a product, selling your company to a prospective "down-liner," or helping a member of your down-line make it through a difficult time, you need to know how to listen. The personality type that we think of as a "typical salesperson" is actually a lousy listener. You will know immediately if you meet one of these people because they will tell you they have the answer to your problem before you even finish a sentence. Sometimes they make successful salespeople because the customer just wants to shut them up, so he or she buys the product!

Good listeners, on the other hand, gain business because they truly understand what someone is looking for. For example, if someone comes to you and says she hates springtime because there is so much gardening work to do, it's your job to find out if she just likes to complain, is looking for sympathy, likes to talk about her hobby, or has real concerns you can help her with (such as providing the hand lotion that keeps her hands from getting chapped when working outdoors).

You know you are a good listener if the following points apply to you:

- "Why" is your favorite question.
- You never change the subject to talk about your problems.
- You naturally understand what someone is feeling even if you have never experienced the same problem.
- People just drop by to talk to you—all the time.
- You rarely tell someone what to do.
- You nod your head and say, "I know," several times in even a short conversation.

ESSENTIALS

Listening doesn't necessarily mean being silent while the other person talks. It means actively listening for their problems and concerns; it means asking questions and knowing what clues signal a true need. Good listeners don't try to get ahead of the discussion.

Creativity

There are very few rules in network marketing (other than business laws that everyone must follow), so when it comes to prospecting for new members of your down-line or trying to break into a new community with your product, it takes creativity to figure out what will work. This is true of any business, but it is even truer in network marketing.

Yes, you might have the only network-marketing company that sells unbreakable china sets, but every one of your customers has access to dishes through a multitude of sources. They may be breakable, they may be more expensive, but they are still dishes. And that's only if the customer needs dishes desperately. If your customer doesn't need dishes, everything else that he or she could possibly spend money on becomes your competition.

The same is true if you're trying to convince someone to join your down-line. If someone is truly looking for a network-marketing opportunity, they are probably going to explore more options than the one you offer. You will be competing with 100-year-old companies that offer well-known products as well as brand-new companies that have never-before-seen items for sale.

It's your job to break through all that clutter with your creativity. Fortunately, you can learn how to be creative. It's as simple as thinking about all the options available to answer a question and knowing that "different" means "good" if it gets the attention you want. If you think you aren't creative, turn to your local college. Most offer courses in building creativity.

FACTS

Creative people know how to think outside the box. They never do something because it's always been done that way. They are always on the lookout for new and better ways to do something, and they are not afraid to give new ideas a try.

Willingness to Learn

Some people like to rest on their laurels. They've worked hard their whole life and want to do what they can with the knowledge they have. That's great—there are plenty of opportunities for self-employment for these personalities. These people make great consultants. They do well when they "step back" a few levels and take a job that they are overqualified for (for instance, magazine editors frequently become freelance writers in their later years).

However, the personality that wants to take a miniretirement won't make it in network marketing. No matter how well-versed you are in business strategies and sales techniques, you undoubtedly know just a small fraction of what you need to become a success in network marketing. You must be willing to learn.

Many people like to learn new things, but that isn't necessary to be successful in network marketing. You don't have to *like* studying, but you do need to recognize its value, because you will be asked to learn new product lines, new business strategies, and new ways to motivate people.

Ability to Live Your Job

One of the biggest personality traits you need to be a success in network marketing is to be able to live your job. Most people like to work set hours and spend the rest of the time doing what they want. Network marketers, however, are always open for opportunities. They are respectful of the fact that others don't necessarily want them to talk about their business all the time, but if the subject comes up, they jump at the opportunity to make a sale.

SSENTIALS

If you are a workaholic, someone who spends ten or more hours a day, six days a week, at work, network marketing may not be right for you. You need to learn to live your job without letting the job take over your life. Otherwise you will quickly burn out.

This is harder than you might think. It means cultivating an understanding with family members that the most routine event—a family dinner, a soccer game, a band concert—could turn into a business meeting. It means the family has to understand that if you took the day off to go to the local amusement park with the kids, you might have to work late into the night when you get home.

The ability to live your job also means you personally have to be flexible. Let's say you were really looking forward to a weekend away from work so you took the family to a hotel for two nights. The first night, as you're sitting around the pool, you find yourself talking to another person who starts to become interested in your network-marketing opportunity when you just casually mention what you do for a living. You really don't want to talk about work but you also know you need to. This one person could open up major doors into a new geographic area.

Living your job also means being able to get your work done whether you want to or not. It may be a beautiful spring day and you would love to be in the garden, but if orders are due, you need to get them done. Yes, network marketing can provide a great deal of flexibility, but you still need to do the work.

If you can't handle the constant pressure to be working—and if you can't find a way to balance work and personal life a minute at a time— you probably won't like network marketing. You will too often feel that you are doing either too much or not enough.

Ability to Put Worry Aside

If you rely on a regular income for your basic needs, perhaps you should reconsider getting involved in network marketing. If you tend to worry about money, you should probably seek a more conventional job.

The reason you can't be a worrier and survive in network marketing is that there is too much to worry about. Network marketing is inherently unpredictable. Until your down-line is firmly established, you won't be able to predict how much money is coming in every month. That you will have bad months is a given.

You also have no control over the fluctuations of the marketplace. You can't control a recession that forces people to cut back on their purchases. You can't control a sudden increase in distributors whose new business contacts cut through your group of prospects. You can't control your company, which may encounter problems with its products.

If you tend to worry about little things over which you have no control—will it rain tomorrow, will the mail get there on time, and so on—you probably are too much of a worrier to enjoy network marketing.

Flexibility

No two days are ever the same for a network marketer. You must be able to move from one thing to the next in a split second. You need to be a visionary and an order-taker at the same time. You need to be able to give a product presentation while searching the audience's personalities for likely distributor candidates.

Some people enjoy knowing what their day is going to be like. They want to know exactly what is expected of them and how they are expected to achieve it. They don't want any surprises. These people are not network marketers.

However, there are others who are energized by the unknown. They find the "same old thing" the biggest demotivator there is. They need the excitement of constant change to feel alive. These people make good network marketers. But not great ones.

The catch is that life in network marketing isn't always new and different. There is some drudgery. You have to fill out forms, make new business calls, and produce mailings. There is no getting around that. As a result, you also have to be flexible enough to be able to do all the unexciting parts of the job.

FACTS

Flexible people know that life isn't all excitement. They look for jobs that offer a balance of tasks that they really enjoy and duties that they don't mind doing when they need to relax a bit. They take pride in being able to do the menial tasks and handle their role as the company visionary.

The Value of Communication

Business is about communication; while we know good communication is important in large corporate settings, many people forget that it can be even more important in other types of business—network marketing is no exception. You will need to communicate with your down-line, your up-line, your customers, and even the people at the home office.

If you are not a good communicator, you likely will fail in network marketing. You will become stuck in a quagmire of "I didn't know" and "You didn't tell me." Your down-line won't know what's going on and people at all levels of the organization will simply think you don't care about the business. You can be working 100-hour weeks but if you don't communicate, you won't make any progress.

If you believe in the value of communication, you will recognize the signs in yourself. You like to tell people what you're up to, you hate secrets, and you feel you should know everything that's going on, too (although you understand that sometimes you can't know everything until the time is right). You're not a good communicator if you believe your privacy is the most important thing there is, if you hate to tell other people what you are doing, and if you see memos and reports as a waste of time.

A Chance at Financial Freedom

Financial freedom is a strong motivator in our culture. It gives you the sense of basic security necessary to do what you like to do, whether it's traveling, buying a new house, sending your kids to college, or even getting involved in other business ventures.

There is no doubt that a good network-marketing program and a healthy dose of perseverance can yield financial security. A few people become millionaires in less than five years. Many more reach their less-lofty financial dreams in a decade or so. Still others pursue the opportunity part-time as an excellent way to have additional income for travel, saving toward their kids' college tuition, or that rainy day that they want to be prepared for.

More Leisure Time

With network marketing you can work when you want and where you want. Do you have a cabin you like to visit in the summer? That's just another opportunity to build a larger down-line. Are you a night worker? That's a good time to do all the paperwork. Looking for a little part-time money to supplement your full-time job? Weekends and evenings are great for network marketing.

Don't be fooled by some sales pitches. Network marketing is still a job. You still have to work to achieve your goals. However, you can decide how hard you will work, leaving you free to pursue your leisure activities when and how you want.

Some people even find that they enjoy network marketing so much that it doesn't seem like work. They are energized by meeting new people and talking passionately about their product. If that's the case with you, you might have just found a way to spend your whole life in leisure!

Even if you find yourself working hard at first, keep in mind that as your down-line grows geometrically, you can reap the rewards of ever-increasing sales with much less effort on your part.

Bringing a Family Together

With crazy sports schedules, school activities, television, computers, and everything else to distract our children, it's no wonder families find themselves drifting apart. However, network marketing can bring a family closer together. What better way to teach children the value of a dollar than to have them see exactly how you earn every penny? What better way to get to know your youngster and have some serious talks about life than while you're stuffing envelopes or delivering your latest orders?

Many successful network marketers say they pursued this opportunity because they wanted a business in which the family could work together. They wanted a chance to learn who their children really are and to help guide them for more than a few minutes a day.

Although money is a wonderful goal, it alone does not bring happiness. Before you get involved in network marketing, examine your reasons closely. If you plan to find happiness because you will have more money and more time for leisure, you will likely be disappointed. If you feel it is something in which you can use all your unique abilities to the utmost, it is a good fit.

CHAPTER 4

Working for Yourself

Human beings are social animals, and it may be very difficult for some people to work by themselves. In network marketing, you have to do everything yourself—from licking the stamps to developing a multifaceted business plan—but you are doing it all *for* yourself. When it comes to this business, you know you are the one benefiting from all your hard work.

Managing Your Time

Because you are on your own, you get to set your own schedule, and network marketing offers plenty of flexibility. Often, people see this as an advantage: You decide when you work and when you play. Finally, you can build work around your life, and not the other way around.

However, flexibility has its downside as well. Flexibility may lead to procrastination. Because no one is forcing you to get the work done, you might never get around to doing it—and all those potential millions remain out of your reach.

If you are a flexibility junkie, you will need to be extremely committed to working for yourself. You will need to set a specific schedule and stick to it. You will have to see your network-marketing venture as a "real" job, even if you are planning to spend just a few hours a week at your new business.

The Workaholic Tendency

Some people are so energized by working for themselves (or so terrified that they won't be able to pay next month's bills) that all they do is work. They end up working eighteen-hour days, holed up in a small corner of their house, never leaving to see their children or to have any fun.

This is a very serious problem. You may make excuses for yourself, explaining that your work is your hobby, or promising yourself to slow down once you start seeing the real money. Unfortunately, the pattern becomes so ingrained that you continue to work long after you have enough money, long after your grandchildren are grown, and long after you have any memory of what it's like to take some free time with family and friends.

How to Avoid Becoming a Workaholic

Examine your behavior. Do you stay up all night working on a personal or business project? Do you tell your family you'll take a vacation "as soon as work slows down," but find that you haven't taken a vacation in the last ten years? Do you say you love to work and call people lazy if they don't work on weekends?

You can avoid overworking by setting as rigorous a schedule for personal time as the ones flexibility junkies need for their work time. Guarantee your family two nights a week. Always break for dinner. Make sure that you have one nonbusiness lunch a week with a friend. Schedule a workout session in the middle of the day. Take one day a weekend to stay completely away from work.

 Another tactic if you're at risk for becoming a workaholic is to do something you have always wanted to do with your life. Learn to play the piano. Fly model airplanes. Take a woodworking class. These pursuits will remind you that there is more to life than working.

Benefits of a One-Person Office

People who work for themselves also often find that they can cut several hours from their work days because they simply don't have coworkers to bother them. There are no chats about new babies or crazy bosses. There are no long lunches for birthdays or half-day retirement parties to take you away from work that you want to get done. You are in control of your day and every minute within that day.

Yet another reason you can save time is that you don't have to deal with as much bureaucracy. Sure, you likely have some forms to fill out every month for the company—to order product or supplies, for example—but you can set up a filing system that works for you. You can wait to file everything once a month, for example, or you can hire your teenager to do the work you hate. There is no "Mickey Mouse" work when you're in business for yourself.

More Work in Less Time

Working on your own also lets you put in a forty-hour work week in as few as twenty hours. Think about it a bit. During a typical eight-hour day of work, how much of that time are you working at peak performance and how much of that time are you barely working at all? How much time do you waste just staring into space as you try to get yourself motivated to do the day's work?

When you work for yourself, you can design a day that works perfectly for you. For example, if your "down" time is between 2 and 4 P.M., you can schedule that time to run personal errands or even make the beds. You can schedule work that requires enthusiasm, such as new business calls, for your "up" times. And you can schedule routine activities, such as filling out forms or filing paperwork during the time of day when you feel most relaxed—when you aren't up to working at top speed but not in need of a nap, either.

Many self-employed people fall into the trap of talking on the phone too long because they crave human contact. Set a timer for ten minutes whenever you pick up the phone and end the conversation as soon as possible once the timer goes off. Very rarely does a call need more time than that.

The Changing Cash Flow

While some people like the predictability of a regular paycheck, many people are energized and motivated by the chance to make as much money as they can in any given month. This works especially well if the business is not essential to paying your family's bills. You simply set aside everything—or a percentage of everything—the business brings in for special purchases or events such as vacations or new vehicles.

After you have been in business for a few years, you will likely see some trends in your cash flow. Perhaps you see more sales in the summer months. If that happens for three years in a row, you can probably count on it happening every year. That, in turn, lets you budget your expenses better.

The Pain of Unpredictable Cash Flow

Still, unpredictable cash flow isn't always fun, especially if you need the money. Ask any professional salesperson who has lost a large long-term account. Suddenly your income shrinks and there is nothing you can do about it, at least not in the short run.

This can be a big concern in a network-marketing business because much of your income comes from the sales other people make. If those people decide to quit the business, you aren't getting your portion of their sales. Likewise, if the product has problems, the company goes out of business, or interest in the item simply falls away because it isn't supported by a good marketing plan, your income can suffer.

Consequently, most people wait until they have had several years of stable or growing income before they decide that they have enough to live on. They may save the majority of the money in the meantime or use it for special events and treats. However, until their down-line is large and stable, the income is so unpredictable that few people with families would risk using this as their sole source of money.

Indeed, as long as you revisit the benefits of changing cash flow and don't become tied to earning a large amount of money that may not be there next month, you will be fine. You will even have some fun.

Tax Concerns

Perhaps the biggest concern from the legal side of a small business is making sure that you're doing everything right with your taxes. After all, you know you need to pay taxes, but are you paying the right amount on time and with the right forms? Many people don't find out the answer until they are audited.

FACTS

Use a retirement savings plan as a way to reduce the taxes you pay. A Keogh plan, for example, lets you put away more money on a tax-deductible basis than an IRA. In many cases, you can contribute as much as $30,000 a year to a Keogh.

According to the General Accounting Office, there are more than 200 different IRS forms that pertain to small businesses. Finding out which of these apply to you can be a major headache. In addition, every year the federal government and state governments pass numerous tax law changes. Many of these changes affect small-business owners because the tax system is frequently used to stimulate or hold back the economy.

For this reason, most people who own small businesses rely on a bookkeeper, certified public accountant, or attorney to do their business taxes. If you have an accountant or other qualified person file your taxes, this person's business usually accepts at least some of the liability if something is done incorrectly. More important, however, is the fact that these people are paid to stay current with the laws and regulations.

What to Pay

Every small-business owner—even those who are involved in network marketing part-time and make only a few extra dollars—must pay taxes that include the federal income tax, state income tax, self-employment tax, property taxes, and state sales taxes. By working with a tax preparer, you will find many deductions and special tax rules that apply in each of these areas.

- *Income taxes.* As you may have discovered already, income taxes aren't as simple when you're in business for yourself. In some cases, losing money is good, because you can deduct it from your taxes. Most of your other expenses, such as entertainment, will be deducted from your income taxes. Remember that your insurance coverage is also deductible from your business income tax.
- *Sales tax* laws vary by state. However, in some cases you won't need to pay sales tax for the products you buy, only for the products you sell. For example, you are exempt from paying sales tax in many states if the item you are buying is an "input" to a finished product on which sales tax will be collected when it is sold. Jewelry makers, for example, don't pay sales tax on the beads they use to make the jewelry.
- *Property taxes* are another area that can become confusing for small-business owners. Any structure used solely for business purposes, as well as the land on which it resides, is definitely property. But capital equipment, such as your computer and your vehicles, is considered

property as well. In these cases, you can depreciate them over several years or take them as a one-time deduction.

- *Self-employment tax.* This tax is probably the most frustrating to new network marketers. If you are in business full-time for yourself, you must pay all of your own social security taxes.

If you plan to deduct any of your business expenses on your taxes, you must then file taxes as a business. The IRS looks askance at people who make these deductions and then claim that their business is just a hobby and they aren't trying to make a profit from it.

Periodic Payments

As an employee of a company, you often don't pay attention to the taxes being withdrawn from your check until the first quarter of the year when you likely have a tax preparer tell you how much you owe or how much you are receiving back from the government.

Life isn't quite so simple when you're self-employed. The federal government and many states demand that you make periodic tax payments four times a year. These are called "estimated taxes" because they don't take into account every deduction.

If you expect to owe more than $1,000 in taxes when you file your federal income tax return, you probably need to make quarterly estimated payments to the federal government using Form 1040-ES. If you don't do this, you could be fined.

Tax Advantages for the Self-Employed

You may have heard that there are many tax advantages to being self-employed. The federal tax code is extremely friendly to small-business owners. Most states also offer tax advantages in terms of deductions and sometimes even tax credits.

Home-Office Deduction

The home-office deduction is perhaps the biggest tax benefit you will see with your home business. It allows you to deduct as a business expense the costs of operating and maintaining the part of your home that you use for business. However, you must meet specific criteria as established by the IRS. A specific area of your home must be used exclusively for your business and it must be used on a regular basis as your principal place of business.

If you use part of your home for inventory or sample storage, you can also take advantage of the home-office deduction. For example, you may grow your business to the point that you decide to rent a small office in a nearby office complex. However, you still use your entire basement to store inventory. The basement area can be used for a tax deduction, even though it isn't your principal place of business.

FACTS

Many people believe that taking a home office deduction raises a red flag with the IRS and makes it more likely that you will be audited. The IRS denies this and, indeed, it appears that the IRS doesn't spend a great deal of time tracking down small-scale abuses of this.

When you meet these criteria, you are able to deduct many expenses from your taxes. For example, all your phone calls and office supplies can be deducted. In addition, you can also deduct a portion of indirect expenses. The actual amount is usually determined by finding the proportion of space in your house actually dedicated to the home office and using that percentage for the deductions. These indirect business expenses include:

- Rent or mortgage
- Heat, air conditioning, and electricity
- Housekeeping
- Security system
- Household supplies such as toilet paper
- Trash collection
- Association fees

Other Deductions

The self-employed person can also deduct items used exclusively for business. In some states, you can deduct a portion of costs for services that are not used exclusively for business, such as a percentage of the costs of Internet service for business and personal use.

Other deductions you may be able to take advantage of include:

- Phones, answering machines, fax machines
- Postage costs
- Health insurance
- Auto expenses, including payments or rental fees, mileage, and insurance
- Business travel
- Office furniture
- Tuition for business-related classes and workshops
- Retirement plans
- Interest on business-only credit cards

Tax Benefits of Hiring Family

Yet another tax benefit can come in terms of hiring your family members. By doing this, you can literally shift income to a lower tax bracket. For example, let's say junior just turned sixteen and wants a new car. You could buy it for him and make the payments. You could make him get a job flipping hamburgers. Or you could hire him for your business, perhaps stuffing envelopes, and pay him a reasonable wage. He will pay less tax on that money than you would because he makes so little money in a year.

You also can hire junior as an independent contractor, which means you don't have to pay any of his social security taxes. You will want to check with your accountant or business lawyer for the exact criteria but, basically, as long as you hire the person for short-term projects and not on an ongoing basis, the person will qualify as an independent contractor.

As an additional benefit, this means junior is actually running his own business, too. Perhaps he offers his envelope-stuffing services to others in your down-line. Then he can take advantage of any business expenses he incurs.

This can be very effective in terms of hiring a stay-at-home spouse. He or she can take care of the children and work on the business a few hours a day. This lets you shift some of your earnings to other family members, meaning you pay less tax and the family members get money you probably would have given them anyway.

Insurance Concerns

If you decide to quit your job and run your network-marketing business full time, you will also need to consider your insurance. You will need several types of insurance that protect both your business and yourself in case something happens.

Do not assume your homeowner's insurance is adequate for your business. Sit down with a professional insurance agent to review all items in your current policies and look for new policies you may need.

The types of insurance that protect your business-related possessions include the following:

- *Fire insurance.* Check your homeowner's insurance to see if the fire coverage pertains to a business run out of your home. If it doesn't, remember that you will need to replace essentials such as a computer system and items that you have for sale in the event of a fire.
- *Theft, vandalism, and malicious mischief insurance.* This type of insurance protects against being robbed or vandalized. Interestingly, many homeowner's plans do not cover the theft of business items. Also, many will have large deductibles for every piece of equipment lost or will give you only the current value of the equipment, not the

replacement value. You want to ensure that your coverage allows you to be back in business tomorrow.

- *Extended coverage insurance.* This covers events such as floods, tornadoes, and smoke damage. Many policies have large deductibles in these areas; you might want to revisit your coverage information to make sure it is adequate for your business.
- *Auto insurance.* You will need special coverage if you have vehicles used for business. In many cases, your rates on auto coverage may increase because you will be driving more miles. On the other hand, if you do most of your business over the phone, your vehicle insurance could go down when you start working full-time from home. Also check to make sure you are covered for products that might be destroyed in an accident.

If your family relies on the business for its livelihood, you should also consider business interruption insurance. This insurance provides a portion of your typical earnings if the business can't operate because of an event such as a flood or tornado. However, be aware that most of these policies take effect only after a certain number of days.

Liability Insurance

As a general rule, you won't need a great deal of liability insurance because your company will carry most of it. However, there are a few items you will want to be insured for. For example, you want basic liability coverage in case someone coming to your place of business has an accident, such as falling down the stairs. This is probably included in your homeowner's policy, but it's best to make sure.

Likewise, you will want to be protected for product liability and professional liability. Though you may think that only large corporations need this type of insurance coverage, that's actually not the case at all.

Product liability can come in handy: If you sell a product that causes damage to a consumer, you (as well as your company) may be held liable. Professional liability applies to those who give advice to consumers. Virtually every network-marketing professional is in the role of making a recommendation at some point. Basic coverage won't be expensive and could save many headaches.

Personal Insurance

Just as you want to protect your business, you need to protect yourself as the business's major employee. Large corporations have "key employee" insurance on their top executives because the business can't function without these people. Think of yourself as your business's key employee and you will see why you need to examine your insurance needs carefully. Then, consider the following types of personal insurance:

- *Health insurance.* This is possibly your biggest concern if you have a family. However, many network-marketing companies offer basic health insurance to their members. Some states offer health insurance to the self-employed. In addition, some insurance companies will offer group plans if you can gather several self-employed people together.
- *Life insurance.* This is relatively easy to get through an independent insurance agent. You might not get as good a deal as you would through an employer, but a basic term policy shouldn't cost too much. Note that if you have a bad health history, you may have been covered in a group plan but find that you can't get coverage as a private individual.
- *Disability insurance.* Many people swear that short-term and long-term disability insurance are even more important than health insurance because they keep bringing in income if you are disabled. The problem is that these insurances can be extremely costly, especially if you have a history of health problems.

FACTS

If you are running a network-marketing business, you could easily consider your business your disability insurance. After just a few years you should have enough residual income coming in to compensate if you become disabled. Plus, with the flexibility offered by being self-employed, you will likely still be able to work a few hours a week to keep growing your business.

CHAPTER 5

Finding the Right Product

Network marketing has gotten a bad reputation because some people get involved in selling bad products. They find a gadget that seems to work great and has a great price tag, sign up to sell it, and suddenly the product is found to be a sham. When you decide to get involved in network marketing, you need to invest some time in looking for a good product that you can genuinely support and that will help your business to grow.

Research Potential Products

There is no secret to doing good business research. It is just a matter of being thorough and looking into every aspect of the product. In some cases, it is as simple as using common sense. In others, it might take a little research on the Internet or a few phone calls.

No matter how long it takes you, though, doing the research to find a good product is very important. A bad product will quickly frustrate you and could even leave you with liability lawsuits. A good product, on the other hand, will be the cornerstone that grows your business into the future.

This is not the time to trust your friends. You must evaluate each product on its own merits and in terms of your needs. If you go into a direct-selling opportunity simply because a friend talks you into it, you're making your first bad business decision.

As you do your research, you will find that better products will generally have more information available on them. That's because the company isn't afraid to talk about these items and because the marketplace is genuinely excited about them, whether they are years old or brand new.

Rely on Your Experience

The first step in the market analysis is to simply look around you and get a feel for the product's potential. Is the product interesting to you? Will you use it on a continuing basis? Does it seem like an item that will be around for a long time or does it appear to be a passing fad? Do you hear people talking about similar products and have you read articles in magazines about this type of item becoming popular?

Let's take herbal remedies as an example. Everyone is talking about them. They are gaining in popularity across the globe. With all the attention on side effects of prescription drugs, most people are at least mildly interested in them. More and more magazine articles appear on the subject every day. If you can think of several people off the top of your head who might buy them, or who already buy them through a retail store, you can probably proceed to the next step in the product research process.

Ask Your Friends and Family

A good way to evaluate the market for the product is to ask your potential sponsor for several product brochures and show them to your family and friends. Ask everyone for their opinions about the products and the prices.

Also ask them what they look for in products like this. For example, if you are looking to sell a line of cutlery products, find out what's more important to your potential customers—the cost, quality, or a warranty? Every person has different reasons for buying something, but you want to know what your future customers are looking for.

It's important to tell your family and friends that you aren't asking them to buy from you—yet. Explain that you want their honest opinion of how well the item would sell and whether they might consider buying it.

Work with the Company

The company that wants you to sell its products should be able to tell you about the items and how well they are expected to sell. Ask for market research information, including magazine articles and anything else the company has that would inform you of the product's place in the market.

In addition, the company should have information about its customers. Look for data that detail the age, sex, income bracket, and geographic region of the customers to help gauge who you will be selling the product to.

Evaluate the Market

Any good businessperson knows that there must be a market for your product if you're going to make any sales. And even if you plan to spend most of your time recruiting new distributors, product must be sold to someone at some point or no one will make any money.

There is a great deal of leeway within that statement. The more money you make per item, the fewer items you will need to sell. On the other hand, if the item is the type of product that is in frequent use and is easy to sell, such as cleaning supplies, a lower price point per each item can still help you to make big profits.

The One-Time Buy

A few years ago a network-marketing company was offering a product that would clean clothes in a washing machine without soap and that would supposedly last for 100 years. This product was later exposed as a fraud, but even if it had worked, where's the potential? After everyone in the world bought one of these gadgets, there'd be no buyers left for the next 100 years.

You want a product that has a growing audience. For this reason, you likely want a company that offers a wide range of items that meet the needs of many different people.

Look for product lines that can grow with the person. If you sell beauty aids, for example, the product line should include items that appeal to teenagers, adults, and the elderly. Your customers will gradually change what they order as the years go by, but they will remain loyal to you and your product line.

On the other hand, if your product appeals only to one small group of people—such as teenage girls—you must constantly search out new customers. Granted, girls are turning thirteen every day, but even the most conservative businesses estimate that it costs three times as much to get a new customer as to keep the one you already have.

A Fair Price

Examine the products closely and see how they stack up for price against items in the retail sector. Look at the general range of products and see if yours falls somewhere in between the low and high ends.

Be careful to look at the quality of the product, because that can significantly change the price. For example, children's educational materials can vary widely in price. If you have definite proof that the item you are considering is high quality, it's fine that it falls toward the high end of the price spectrum.

The Dangers of Saturation

Network-marketing companies love to tell you that there is no such thing as market saturation. Not true. Every product and every type of company has its limits. A marketplace can handle only so much. Look at any retail operation as confirmation of this. Examples are everywhere; for instance, chances are you won't see two hardware stores on the same block in your town.

If you find that there is more than one distributor for every 5,000 people within a thirty-mile radius of you, it's a sign to look a little further at the market for this product. It's not necessarily bad news if the item has a number of strengths, but it could signal saturation.

You can find some signals that the product might be overextended in the marketplace by asking the parent company for a list of (or at least the number of) active distributors in your town or county. If you feel there are too many, ask the company how it plans to deal with market saturation.

Market saturation isn't a problem if you have reason to believe you can break out of your region by recruiting new distributors. You may have a healthy number of friends and relatives in another state who you are certain would become distributors. Or you might have connections via a vacation home or another hobby that takes you to many different parts of the country. For example, people who participate in dog shows may also be network marketers, using their dog-show trips as fuel for their network-marketing business.

Is the Marketplace Changing?

Many a network marketer has gotten caught in a changing marketplace. A good parent company, of course, will be aware of any changes and alter their product line accordingly. However, some simply continue to believe in the same old thing.

Read trade magazine articles in the general area of the product and try to determine what is happening in the industry. Are you thinking of selling a clothing line? Oops, the items are made of 100 percent polyester and trends say people are looking for blends or natural fabrics—it could be a tough sell in the near future. All it takes to find out about these trends is a bit of reading.

ESSENTIALS

A librarian can direct you to many research studies that will tell you what is happening in any marketplace. Try to find signals of major changes, like dramatic drops in consumer spending in a particular product category.

Also, do research at the library to determine if your potential market is growing or shrinking. If your product appeals to aging middle-income people, for example, your market is growing by thousands of people a day. If your product appeals to high-income housewives, you may be in trouble.

Remember that you're looking for long-term information, so don't be too concerned about general economic trends. Yes, if you sell a line of expensive candles or baskets, your sales might go down during a recession, but a strong, good-quality product will survive. In fact, many expensive items actually see increased sales during recessions because people will buy only what they know is good; they don't want to gamble with their limited funds.

If the product is totally unique and has no competitors in the retail sector, it is very likely fraudulent. The sign of a good product is that it has good competitors. They don't have to be as good as your item, but they should provide a comparable function.

Do You Like Your Customers?

The customer is an important part of the decision for virtually any product you might consider. You may have determined that the item has a wide market available to it, but for some reason you aren't attracted to it. That could be because you aren't comfortable with the people you would be selling to.

For example, if you are a fifty-something man who has no children and has been a diesel mechanic for thirty years, you probably wouldn't want to sell children's toys. These products might be something you can believe in, but you likely wouldn't be comfortable with the young mommies you'd be selling to.

Another example is herbal medicines. The popularity of these items is beginning to cross all demographic categories. However, they still tend to be most popular with people who believe in New Age ideas. If you think New Age ideas are stupid and you couldn't care less about cutting down the rainforest, you probably won't like the people you will be selling to.

Sell to Yourself First

Most people decide to sell to people like themselves. That makes sense, because people like you will probably like the product as much as you do. However, you will also have to break out of your group of friends and relatives into the bigger world. Will you like the world that you encounter?

Here is an example: When a popular line of kitchen utensils started network marketing, a retired chef living a modest lifestyle in the country decided to join in. His first customers were professional and amateur gourmet chefs, and his work ran smoothly. However, eventually he realized that he needed a larger base of customers. The more typical customer base for the items he was selling turned out to be young urban professionals. It was then that our chef found out that he really didn't like working with these people.

FACTS

Remember, you can't like everybody. You're bound to have customers you don't care for as friends. However, you want to make sure that you agree with your typical customer's outlook on life, including his or her morals and values. If you don't, it will quickly show in your sales.

Looking to Alternatives

At the same time, you may see a big opportunity that other distributors for the company have missed. Perhaps you can see that a large segment of people would be interested in the product line but have never been approached about it.

For example, some houseware distributors have made large sales to relatively poor college students who were starting to think about setting up their own households. Another decided to sell to the young gay men's market after her brother became enthusiastic about the products. One beauty supply salesperson hit the drag queen marketplace. Another went to breast cancer support groups, noting that people in chemotherapy frequently seek ways to look more beautiful. A toy salesperson went to elderly housing complexes and pitched the items as perfect gifts for grandchildren. An herbal remedy salesperson sold to nurses and doctors at her workplace, convincing them that they needed to at least try what their patients were considering.

If you think you might have an alternative customer base for your product, ask a few other distributors what they think. Find out if the company has ever approached these groups and what happened. Most importantly, look to these groups for advice. Visit them with product brochures before you make your decision.

A Product You Believe In

According to the Direct Selling Association, the second most common reason people go into network marketing is that they believe the product is good. (The first reason, not surprisingly, is to make money.) You are betting your future on this product, so it's critical that you believe in it. Yes, you can make some sales of an item that you don't believe in, but your attitude will soon catch up with you and people won't be enthusiastic because they will sense your disinterest.

In fact, perhaps the best way to select your network-marketing company is to look at the products you currently use. If you are totally dedicated to one company's product line, that's likely the one for you. Even if the market is fairly saturated and the product's growth potential isn't the best, you can overcome these barriers with your enthusiasm.

If you don't have the opportunity to find out about a wide range of products, simply start asking around. Suddenly you'll find network-marketing opportunities coming out of the woodwork. Friends of friends will call you. You will find ideas online. You will even meet network marketers that are trying to sell you their products. Simply try the most intriguing items for a couple of months and see which ones you can truly support.

A Product's Complexity

In today's consumerist world, you can always find a few people who will buy from you on blind faith, but Ralph Nader and his followers have made more and more people skeptical about everything they purchase. They want to know why a product works and how it works. Even if a product is well established in the marketplace, you will need to answer new questions.

For example, forty years ago no one even thought about whether eye shadow was tested on animals, was made from natural products, or was hypoallergenic. If it made the user break out, she just stopped using it.

Likewise, people weren't as concerned with health products. They would give anything a try once, especially if a friend recommended it. Remember how popular it was to wear copper bracelets for arthritis, even though physicians never recommended it? Today, many of your customers would want to know why copper relieves arthritis pain and whether there are any medical studies that support this claim. If you can't supply a good answer, you probably won't make the sale.

The company that supplies your product should give you an explanation of why its products work, but is it understandable? Do you personally understand the physiology of pain relief and why magnets help, for example? Do you understand why all-natural soap is better than soap containing man-made chemicals?

And, even more important, can you explain this easily and quickly to a customer, or do you find yourself just accepting that "it's technical"? If you personally don't understand how and why the product works, it's best to pass it by, lest you get sucked into a scam.

 **SSENTIALS** Try to explain the product to a ten-year-old child, then ask the child to explain it to someone else. While the child may not remember all the details, the general explanation should match yours. If it works, you know you can explain the complexity of your product to anyone.

You don't have to be a scientist to provide good explanations. They just have to make sense. For example, one company sells microwaveable pouches that provide heat for aching muscles. Complete textbooks have been written on pain relief but all you need to know is that heat causes blood to rush to the area and the increased blood flow relieves the pain.

When Quality Is the Point

Perhaps even more difficult to explain is how your product is better in quality than a competing item. Plus, you have to explain why that higher quality matters.

Let's say, for instance, that you are selling a line of children's toys. You might say that these toys are better in quality than 80 percent of the toys on the marketplace because they are made of thick plastic in bright colors so they last longer—in fact, you can stand on them and they still wouldn't break. That's great, your customer would say, but why should I care? In a few months, my child won't want to play with the toy anyway.

How do you respond? Well, you point out that higher quality means the child is less likely to get hurt by sharp edges resulting from broken toys. And the bright colors mean the toys won't get lost as easily in the yard or at the beach.

Another company sells inexpensive fragrances and beauty supplies. It doesn't have a "quality" message. Or does it? The quality in this company's product is actually the word "quantity." Customers can try out many different products for a low price until they find the ones they like. Add to that a quick delivery system and an open-ended return policy, and many customers see quality where you thought there was none.

Performing a SWOT Analysis

A SWOT analysis evaluates strengths, weaknesses, opportunities, and threats of a particular product. Professional salespeople and marketers frequently perform SWOT analyses when they are trying to decide on their sales or marketing strategies. This same tactic can help you decide if a product is right for you.

FACTS

To carry out the analysis, you first need to gather all the information you can about the product, its market, its consumers, and the trends that indicate how well it will sell in the future. Then, look at the four areas of SWOT and write down what you see.

Strengths

Strengths can come in many different forms. They can be tangible (like, the product comes in a sturdy plastic bottle) or intangible (like, the product has been in use for more than forty years). Strengths include—but are not limited to—all of the product benefits the parent company likely has supplied you with.

Generally, a strength is anything that makes the item easier to sell. To find the product's strengths, go through all the information you have gathered and decide what might make someone decide to buy this product if all other factors were equal between it and a competing item. In particular, consider the following:

- *A well-known name.* This means you don't have to inform your customers about the product. A proven brand name is generally preferable over an unknown one, even if the unproven product is a better value. This is the reason name-brand groceries sell better than store brands. They're the same item, but people like to buy the name they know.

- *Duration.* The product has been around for several decades. It's apparently versatile and can meet different needs. It's recently become popular to "rediscover" old products, especially in the home, personal care, and wellness product categories. (Many product companies such as Coke and Hershey are reintroducing their "classic" products and packaging.)

- *Performance.* If the product is proven to perform better than all of its competitors in nonbiased scientific studies, there is little to argue with here. Scientific evidence that your product works better than another one is very convincing sales information.

- *Price.* If the product is relatively low priced, many people will give it a try—even if they aren't convinced that it's better. If the product is high priced, it might appeal to a smaller group, but you will get a higher commission for each item you manage to sell. Some people want the prestige of buying the top of the line and it'll be easier to sell high-priced items to them.

- *Quality.* High quality means good value for the money. For example, if you can show that while your laundry detergent costs twice as much as the supermarket brand, it will clean three times as much laundry, you have quality as a strength.

- *Environmentally friendly.* A growing number of people are interested in the environment and the negative health effects of man-made chemicals; these people will be interested in purchasing products that are all-natural and have not been tested on animals. And the other folks certainly won't see this as a weakness.

- *Packaging.* Packaging makes products look more expensive, so your customers will feel they are getting more value for their money. In addition, you won't have to deliver beaten-up boxes to your customers or worry about customers hurting themselves on broken bottles.
- *Media attention.* If the product category is getting a lot of attention in the press, you'll have an easier time educating your customers about the benefits of your item.

QUESTIONS?

What if something seems like it's both a strength and a weakness?
That's actually very common. List it in both categories and then examine it more closely to determine if it's a strength for one type of customer and a weakness for another type; then use your analysis accordingly when you're selling.

Weaknesses

Weaknesses are anything that might make the product difficult to sell. Interestingly, what is perceived as a strength in one product can be a weakness in another.

- *A well-known name.* This means people have preconceived ideas about the product. If those ideas are negative, you'll have a harder time changing the consumer's mind than if you had to educate him or her from the beginning.
- *Old news.* The product has been around for several decades and might be perceived as being old-fashioned and out of date.
- *Price.* If the product is relatively low priced, people might think it lacks quality and is not worth trying. If the product is high priced, people might think it's not worth their money.
- *Use.* It's difficult to sell items that people rarely use, especially if these are high-quality items. For example, most people wouldn't splurge on

a $40 cheese slicer that they might use once or twice a month. At that rate, a $4 cheese slicer will last a whole lifetime, too.

• *An innovation.* If the product is new to the marketplace, you will need to educate consumers about it, and you will run into skepticism. You also run the risk that the item won't live up to its claims.

Opportunities

Opportunities are created by what is happening in the marketplace, and they make your product easier to sell in the future. Consider these examples of market opportunities:

• *More people are becoming conscious of the value in herbal remedies and "natural" products.* If your product is "all natural," that's a definite opportunity.
• *The population of the United States is growing older.* If you have an item that appeals to older people, this is a definite opportunity.
• *People are waiting until their thirties to have children.* If you sell expensive toys and educational materials, this is to your advantage because older parents have more disposable income.
• *A recession is on the horizon.* If your product is a good value, it may actually see increased sales during a recession, because in lean times people don't like to take risks. This is also the chance to talk about the company's direct-delivery policy and Internet ordering system, both time-savers for the busy two-worker household.

FACTS

Opportunities and threats may be specific to your location. Search your local paper to see if any events are about to alter your community. Examine the demographics and values of people you will be selling to before you decide if a trend is an opportunity or a threat.

Threats

Threats can refer directly to an individual product or to the company. Like opportunities, frequently they are things that could happen in the future. As a result, they often aren't used to make a decision about whether to sell a product (unless there are so many threats that the idea of getting involved becomes absolutely frightening). For the most part, you want to know what the threats are so you can determine if you and the company are equipped to handle them in the event that they occur.

- *The product line is increasingly popular.* Due to this popularity, competitors are springing up every day in all sectors—from direct sales to retail. You and the company will have to fight harder to convince people why your products are better.
- *The U.S. population is aging.* Eventually this will mean that more people are living on fixed incomes. And if you sell things that appeal to younger folks, you might find this fact a threat.
- *A recession is on the horizon.* If you are thinking of selling a luxury product line, it could be one of the first products consumers cut back on. After all, if the choice is feeding the kids or redecorating the living room, it's apparent which item will lose its foot in the market.
- *The product has not been proven to work from a scientific standpoint.* A consumer group or a research company might discover that, in fact, it does not work at all. If the product fails the examination, your parent company will quickly be out of business.
- *The product has been tested on animals, uses man-made chemicals, or is made in a third-world country.* All of these factors can be hot buttons for large groups of people. Unfortunately, these things can become important with very little warning, jumping from a fringe-group interest to the mainstream almost overnight.

Putting It Together

You can make your SWOT analysis as simple or as detailed as you like. However, the more work you put into it, the more information you will have to help you make a decision about a specific product line.

You will never find the perfect product, but you can minimize your risk by spotting major red flags before you sign up. Plus, learning about the benefits and shortcomings of your product will open your eyes to fresh selling points and untapped customer groups.

CHAPTER 6

Evaluating Potential Companies

It's impossible to choose your product without also looking at the company that you would be working with to distribute it. You want your network-marketing venture to take you to a bright future, so you need to make sure the company you align with has your future in mind, too. Look for a company that is well established and has a sound reason for selling its items through this method.

The Importance of Research

Perhaps the most important part of deciding to go with a specific network-marketing company is knowing that it will be there for you in the future. Times may get slow now and then, but you want a company that is prepared to pull its salespeople through these tough times.

Although it is impossible to predict with certainty the future of any company, you can make some educated guesses based on as much information as you can possibly gather. Make sure you do your research well before you commit your precious dollars and time to a particular venture. There are many ways to do this, and some resources yield more information than others. You want to create a game plan that will get you the most information in the shortest time.

If you are serious about making network marketing your sole source of income some day, plan to spend at least forty hours researching your opportunities. After all, your future should be worth at least one week's work!

First, Make a Short List

Chances are, you have one or two opportunities in mind already. In fact, you are probably considering network marketing because a friend has been successful with a certain product line or because you have been a customer of a particular network marketer for several years.

However, you want to have at least three options. It is fine if you're "all but certain" that one is right for you, but you want to have some other companies to compare your first choice to.

The best place to start is your local library. They should have one or more books that list a number of network-marketing opportunities. You also can reach associations such as the Direct Selling Association through the library computer (unless of course you have a computer at home). Once you get a list of hundreds of network-marketing companies, including their product line and a short history, pick out your front-runner and two others that seem interesting at first glance.

Information You Must Have

As you do your research on these companies, you will want to find out how the company does business, how it treats its employees, how it is regarded in the marketplace, and other relevant information. You want to know what it has done in the past and why.

FACTS

An Internet search on any major search engine should come up with at least five entries for the company's name, including magazine articles, the company's home page, and perhaps mentions in industry listings.

You are looking for facts, to be sure, but you are also looking for feelings. As with any working situation, what can be perfect for many people may not be perfect for you. You want to get a feel for how you would fit in with the company. Even though you will be working on your own most of the time, you will have to deal with these people a fair amount, so you want them to think like you do.

You are also trying to find information that will give you some clue as to how the company will fare in the future. You want to know if it is poised to survive economic and marketplace changes. You also want to know if its management is committed to keeping the company in business in the future. While it's never possible to predict the future, you can gain some clues by looking at how the company handled problems in the past as well as examining new business strategies the company is planning to implement.

Ownership Structure

Find out who owns the company and its prospective ownership structure for the near future. Only a few direct-marketing companies are publicly owned. Most are started by one person or a partnership, who may extend partial ownership to other executives as the company grows. A few are looking to become public companies in the future and offer opportunities for their distributors to gain stock ownership.

The ownership status doesn't have great significance unless you find extremely good or bad news. If the company has grown significantly but is still owned by one person, that gives you a sense of its management priorities. If the company is planning to go public and is offering incentives for salespeople to earn stock, that is a definite plus in your potential income column.

The Financial Situation

If it is a public corporation, you will have access to the annual report as well as other financial documents. Often these are available at the library, or you can always contact the company directly and ask for the report, which will be sent to you free of charge.

Income is not a good predictor of a company's financial standing. (As you know, many wealthy people have filed for bankruptcy, as have many large corporations.) Instead, you want to determine the prospective company's financial stability.

If you are looking at a privately held corporation, you may or may not have access to financial reports. However, a librarian may still help you find reported earnings through federal documents. In some cases, for example, companies can make only certain "lists" if they have specific income.

The annual report and other financial documents will tell you how much debt the company has and will usually include information on why that debt exists and how the company plans to remain solvent in the future.

In the case of a privately owned company, you may want to candidly ask top management about the financial stability of the company. You also could ask former employees or competitors how the company is doing.

Company Ethics

Business ethics has taken a big hit in recent years. And, as we've all discovered, what is ethical to one person may not be to the next. It's important to gain some idea of how the employees of a particular company are encouraged to approach ethical dilemmas.

Are they asked to avoid the subject and just do what the company says, or are they encouraged to bring dilemmas to the attention of management at the home office? Often, ethical dilemmas can be quickly solved with explanations and a look at the applicable laws, but management should always be willing to explain why it works the way it does.

Experienced Executives

Not everyone is cut out for network marketing, so you shouldn't be too surprised if you find that a number of executives at the company you are looking at don't have direct experience in this area of business. However, there are some signs that will point to a strong management team. These include:

- *Most executives have long tenure with the company.* This applies especially to the board of directors and at least half of the vice presidents. Look for a minimum of five years; ten is preferable.
- *The company's leader has a great deal of business experience.* If the president or CEO doesn't have experience with network marketing, he or she should have industry experience.
- *People at the top understand direct sales and network marketing.* They may not have a great deal of experience in the area, but they should know everything there is to know about this business style.
- *Sales executives of this company have experience in network marketing.* This is the one area where you can't slack off. The sales trainers and support team must know what you are dealing with every day.
- *The executives have a broad base of expertise.* Too many network-marketing companies are started by someone with a good idea and a fast-talking sales personality. But beyond that, the business expertise starts to falter. The management team should have a broad base of experience in business areas including marketing, distribution, and product development, as well as in management.

Company Vision and Mission

The company should have a clearly stated vision for its future. Ideally, it should be the first thing you see on written materials from the company, because the vision should be the driving force behind all decisions.

While a vision may come in a variety of forms, it must encompass the company's growth objective and the plan for getting there. For example, your company might say, "We want to be the world leader in supplying herbal nutrients to people through direct sales."

The mission is a more day-to-day tool that is used to help guide the company's employees and distributors as they make routine decisions. Ideally, any question you have about working the business should be answered by turning to the mission. For example, the same company's mission might be, "To provide high-quality, pure herbal nutrients at a fair price with timely delivery." That pretty much tells you what to do every minute you're working!

If the company is ignoring recent technological innovations, you should be concerned about its future. At the minimum, the company should have a Web site that potential customers can visit to find out more about the products and the company's philosophy.

The Roles of Employees and Distributors

While you won't technically be an employee of the company, you will want to know that the company pays a good wage and treats its employees well, because that is a sign of how they will treat their network marketers.

You want to know that the company sees you as the most important person in the business. You are the person who brings in the money that pays the top executives and even the janitors at the home office. As a result, you should be treated like royalty by absolutely everyone in the company.

Delivery and Returns

You should also consider how the company handles the delivery of its products to end users and what the policy is on returns. Many companies will ship items to their distributors, who must then deliver them to their customers; if such is the case, be prepared to spend more time in the car (or at the post office) than if the company ships directly to customers. That isn't all bad because delivering the product yourself gives you another chance to sell to the customer. But remember to add in a delivery fee to cover your gas or if you have to ship the product to the customer yourself.

Return policies vary from company to company as well. Some will accept all returns, no questions asked, but many others won't. If the company does not accept returns, this means you will have to negotiate with your customer for a solution to their dissatisfaction and may end up reimbursing the full price of the product. If the company does accept returns, find out if you are responsible for filling out any forms and how the customer gets his or her money back. These are issues that could affect your workload, especially as your business grows.

It's Time to Begin

Now that you have a good idea of the type of information you want to find out, it's time to start the research process. Some people may find this task overwhelming; others have no trouble getting started but don't know where to stop.

The best tactic is to break the research into three distinct sections: printed information, people associated with the company, and unbiased experts. Create a file for each section of every company you have decided to research; then, start stockpiling information.

QUESTIONS?

What if I can't find any information about the company?
A truly good company with a truly good product or business philosophy is bound to grab the attention of the media, so there should be at least a small article on the company in some publication. Steer clear of companies that have absolutely no publicity.

Printed Information

The library is the best place to go to begin your research. If you don't know how to use today's researching tools, ask a librarian for help. Librarians love to do research and track down obscure facts—and they love to help. By simply asking, you will receive the power of a master's degree in information research. Most librarians will even work on a project for several weeks with you.

If the company is locally based, you might find a special file that includes the company's product brochures. Sometimes you will even find a Ph.D. thesis or other published work that has examined the company you are researching.

You should also be able to get a great deal of printed material from your potential sponsor or from the company directly. This should include detailed product information and general information about the company's history, goals, and structure.

Finally, you may find printed information from industry associations such as the Direct Selling Association. These groups frequently produce directories of their members. Some will have lists of companies in various categories such as sales revenue or even association involvement. A few will even sponsor research into the best companies.

People Associated with the Company

Every company has a number of people associated with it. Current and former customers and distributors (especially your potential sponsor) as well as consultants who have worked with the company can all give you insight about the company you are considering.

ESSENTIALS

Listen closely to people who have decided to part ways with a company. Even stories that sound like sour grapes can tell you a great deal about how a company values people and conducts business on a daily basis.

Simply ask these people what their impressions are of the company. Why do they like it? Why were they or are they associated with it? Why did they break off the association? Would they recommend it? Is there anything you should be concerned about?

An ethical company can help you get in touch with some of these people. In fact, they should be impressed that you are willing to go to this amount of detail in your research, because it shows how committed you are to working hard at the business.

Experts

Business experts come in many forms. Basically, any person who has an unbiased opinion about your prospective company or network marketing in general is an expert. For example, see if you can get in touch with a local community college professor who teaches network marketing or other business courses.

You can also find experts at business and consumer associations. Even an association loosely affiliated with your company's industry can tell you what trends are occurring in the marketplace and provide good questions for you to ask the top management.

Also, don't forget to call the Better Business Bureau and the state attorney general's office to determine if there have been any problems with the company or the products.

Contact the Company Directly

Your research may have turned up a fair number of questions. But even if the company seems very solid, you still want to get a feeling for how it does business and how it treats its distributors. This will mean talking to the people who actually run things. The best way, if you are nearby, is to take a tour of the home office. However, you also can do these chats by phone.

Prepare a list of questions for each person you will be talking to, and keep a notebook for writing down the answers and taking notes. Don't be afraid to ask difficult questions about problems the company had in the past. A good businessperson will be candid about these problems and their solutions.

If company employees seem reluctant to talk to you, pass this opportunity by. At best, it means they won't have time to help you once you sign on. At worst, it could signal any number of business or even legal problems that the company wants to keep secret.

Speaking with the Management

These are the people who decide the direction the company will take in the future and ultimately determine what products the company will sell, how the items will be marketed, how much you make for selling products, and virtually every other decision that affects your future. You want to ask them questions about the entire scope of operations. A few examples include:

- Why does your company rely on network marketing to distribute your products?
- Do you have any plans to change the sales structure?
- Where do you see network marketing going in this product area?
- What is your personal experience with network marketing?
- How are you dealing with market saturation?
- Why did you handle (whatever problems you found) in this way?

What you're looking for is information that makes sense to you. For example, if the CEO says the company uses network marketing so people like you can become millionaires, he's clearly trying to dodge the question. A company uses the sales method it does because it is best for that company. The CEO should be able to tell you why direct selling makes the most sense based on the product and the marketplace.

Likewise, if top management says there is no such thing as market saturation, it's time to ask a few more questions. Any product can become saturated, especially in small geographic areas. The company should have plans in place to introduce more depth or breadth to the product line to counter possible market saturation.

Speaking with the Employees

Manufacturing, delivery, customer service, and clerical workers are the people who actually make the company run. They will be able to tell you about things that will matter to you every day—how likely your product is to be high quality and how likely it is to be delivered correctly and on time.

FACTS

Employees can give you a sense of what the company is like as an employer and how the company views its distributors. If these people have a great deal of respect for the distributors and are happy with their compensation and benefits, it's likely you also will be happy as a distributor.

Ask these people the following questions:

- How is the product made?
- How do you feel about the people who sell the products?
- Why aren't you involved in selling the product yourself?
- How many product recalls do you have in a year?
- Do the product formulations change much?
- Who do I call if I have a delivery problem?
- How soon do you deliver product after an order is placed?
- Do you like working here?
- What's the most common problem you get?

At this point, you're looking for honesty. Nothing is ever perfect, so if it sounds like you're getting "the company line" on a question, ask further. In terms of product and delivery, you want to hear that occasional problems occur but they do their best to straighten them out as quickly as possible. In terms of attitude, you want to hear that they like their jobs and that the distributors are the most important people because they keep the company in business.

Marketing and Product Development People

While top management is focused on the future and the workers are focused on today, the people in product development and marketing are looking to help you sell the products tomorrow. They are responsible for finding new and better items, packaging those products well, and designing the marketing programs that will make the products enticing. You will want to ask them the following questions:

- What new products are in development?
- Why are you going in this direction?
- What marketplace trends are important to the company?
- Why do you think network marketing works for this company?
- What are your most successful promotions?
- Who do you think buys the product?
- How do you decide what products to offer?

Try to determine if the company approaches product development and marketing as a science. It should look at marketplace trends as well as product trends to determine what items to offer in the future. The marketing staff should know exactly who buys the products and why they buy them.

The Sales Support and Training Team

These are the people who will help you get started in direct sales. They will provide the brochures and newsletters you will give to customers. They will also provide your first as well as ongoing sales training. Ask them the following questions:

- What is different about direct sales as compared to other types of sales?
- When was the sales training last modified?
- Whose sales methods are the training materials based on?
- Have you ever worked as a distributor for the company?
- Why are you a sales trainer?
- What other companies have you worked for?
- Why do you work for this company?

Try to determine if the internal sales support staff has the experience and talent to help you become a successful salesperson. You want to find people who have experience in direct sales and know how it differs from other sales strategies. You also want to find people who have experience in other sales settings and have chosen this job because they like direct sales.

Beyond the Hype

Unless you are very lucky, the information you receive will be overwhelmingly positive. Why is that unlucky? Because every company has had problems in its past and you want to be able to discover what those were and how they were handled. Unfortunately, even the most unbiased newspaper or magazine reporter likes to put a positive spin on a story. Employees and industry associations like to be positive. Even competitors and former employees will be reluctant to spread bad information.

Your job, therefore, is to sort through the information to look for holes and inconsistencies. For example, does one article say the company has seen double-digit growth every year for the last ten years while another says it has had modest growth? Does a magazine article allude to five years of stagnant growth? Does the company president repeatedly brush off questions about competition?

Companies have definite personalities that don't change quickly. If a company is secretive today, more than likely it will be tomorrow. If employees see your visit as a bother today, they probably will when you're a distributor, too.

Make a list of everything that seems the least bit unusual. It may not be a problem, but if something seems odd to you, it's definitely something worth researching a little more.

Even more important than the negative information about a company is how the company has handled its problems. Often, companies in trouble will hire a new CEO to help fix things. Look for the business magazine article that talks about the methods a new CEO used to turn the company around one to two years after he or she was hired.

Look for Trends

Your research into the past is a tool for discovering how the company is likely to handle a similar problem in the future. To check for negative trends, chart your prospective company's major events.

No company is free of warts. Look for a company that admits its faults and works to correct them. If the same problem seems to happen again and again, you can bet it will continue into the future.

When It's Time to Make the Decision

While your feelings and emotions should be an integral part of this decision, it's essential to look at your research results carefully before really committing to an opportunity that will determine your future. You don't want to be overly swayed by your potential sponsor or an especially slick company presentation. You want to know that this is the right company for you. Before you commit to a decision, ask yourself the following questions:

- Is this a company I can grow old with?
- Does this company have the expertise to weather market and economic changes?
- Has this company handled itself ethically in the past?
- Are the employees people I could see as friends?
- Do the executives have my best interests in mind?

You may find that the company you thought was fantastic just seemed a little too shaky to bet your future on and decide to do a little more research on other companies. Eventually, though, you will find one company that stands out from all the others. Then, you will know that all that research has paid off, and you can take the next step—network-marketing training.

CHAPTER 7

How You Will Make Money

Every company has a slightly different twist on how it pays its network marketers, but there are some typical components that make a compensation plan fair and reasonable. When it comes to your plan, look at the advantages for newcomers as well as how much work it will take to really start making the big bucks.

The Premise of Network Marketing

The principle behind network marketing is getting paid for other people's work. Every time someone in your network makes a sale, you receive a percentage of that money. That fact gives you the incentive to pick good distributors and train them well. In exchange, you will make money off direct sales made by your trainees as well as everyone in their down-lines. The theory is that everyone in the up-line is helping the person make the sale by communicating their expertise and ideas "down the line" to the person who directly sells to the customer.

ESSENTIALS

As your network grows it's possible that you will have people in your down-line that you have never met. It doesn't matter where they are or what you did (or didn't) do to help them become good distributors. Every time they make a sale, you receive a small percentage of the revenue.

Many network-marketing plans are also front-end loaded, meaning that you receive a large bonus or commission when you bring in a new distributor. For example, you might receive 10 percent of your own sales and a $500 bonus for signing up a new distributor, plus 2 percent of that person's sales. It's easier to find one distributor than to sell $5,000 worth of product, which means this company prefers its distributors to recruit other distributors rather than sell their products.

A true network-marketing program will encourage you to sell some of the products yourself and, like most salespeople, you usually receive the greatest amount of money on sales you actually make. In some organizations this can be as much as 60 percent of the item's price. In the corporate world, a salesperson would have to fill quotas or meet sales goals before he or she received a bonus for good work. In network marketing, you are rewarded immediately for the results of your work.

You also get paid every time one of your customers buys something, even if you never talk to the person. In many network-marketing companies, the customer can phone in an order or order over a Web site. Because you first found this customer, you get credit for the sale even though you didn't really do anything.

Unilevel Plans

The most common type of payment system in network marketing is called a unilevel plan. These plans are usually front-end loaded, paying a nice bonus when you recruit a new distributor, but they also pay well for sales you make yourself.

As a distributor becomes more removed from you—the recruit of a recruit of a recruit, for example—you receive a smaller percentage of their sales. For example, as a new recruit, you might get 25 percent of your sales, 10 percent of your first-line's sales, 8 percent of your second-line's sales, and so on. Eventually you will stop receiving money from the sale of someone far below you, usually at about level seven.

Sometimes these plans pay "generational" bonuses—extra money for the work of a specific generation of recruits below you. For example, if your plan has a third-generation bonus, it offers you a larger percentage of the sales from your recruit's recruit's recruits than from the people you actually recruited. Frequently, these bonuses last a few months, although some companies build them in permanently because they find that it encourages distributors to work with more people in their down-lines.

Perhaps the best part of a unilevel plan is that you truly are the boss of a little business. You don't have to share the income with anyone else, as in some other plans, and your network can continue growing forever.

FACTS

Most compensation plans for legitimate network-marketing opportunities are built upon a unilevel plan but include items unique to the company, such as volume and recruitment bonuses or breakaway options.

Some of these plans also offer the chance to get promoted to a higher job title. Once your down-line begins making a certain level of sales each month or once you have signed on a certain number of distributors, some companies will call you a director, a title that comes with a substantial bonus.

These plans can be fun to work with because there are so many people involved and everyone is encouraging everyone else. The companies frequently sponsor motivational meetings and encourage people to hold their own down-line meetings. A large down-line can actually become like a family as they share ideas for building sales and bringing in more recruits.

Unfortunately, these plans are also the most difficult with which to reach the magic million-dollar mark because you typically need thousands of people below you. Unless you are breaking into a new market where you believe you can literally recruit hundreds of people yourself and that each of those people will be able to recruit many others, you may become frustrated by the small amount of money you can make.

Unilevel payment plans are wonderful if they are the second income in a family or if you are starting the program at a young age and have confidence that the product line has staying power.

Stair-Step Breakaway Plans

A unilevel plan can continue growing forever, even though you typically won't see any money from the sales of people far into your down-line. However, some companies have created an added incentive to recruit distributors by adding what they call a stair-step breakaway.

Although breakaway plans can be motivating to the new distributor, they don't allow you to stop working after several years because you must constantly replace down-line members who have made the break.

These plans are run much like a unilevel plan until you reach certain goals that frequently include a certain number of distributors directly underneath you as well as a certain dollar amount generated in a quarter or a year. When you reach these goals, you gain the right to break away from your sponsor and move up a step in the network, receiving a higher level of commissions. All of your recruits also move up a step.

Frequently, a plan will have two or three chances to "stair climb," thus giving you greater incentive to keep growing your business directly.

These plans are frequently used in programs that encourage selling to other distributors as opposed to selling to new customers. They may require that you buy products up front and sell them to others down the line. The danger, of course, is that you will hit a saturation level for new recruits and be stuck with a garage full of items you couldn't sell.

Another problem with this plan is that the initial sponsor might not want his people to break away. After all, if the distributor has been doing well enough to reach that level, he or she is probably generating a good income for the initial sponsor. Some companies solve this problem by giving a one-time large bonus when a leg breaks away.

Big Bonus Plans

Bonus plans typically operate as unilevel plans but include large bonuses as you reach specific levels of sales yourself or in your network. They might also have rewards for the physical size of your down-line.

One bonus might be for personal sales. For example, you might receive 10 percent of every sale you personally make until you reach $1,000 in sales. After that, you receive 15 percent on everything, including the initial $1,000, until you reach $5,000, where the commission goes to 20 percent.

FACTS

Plans that offer lots of bonuses can be fun because they reward you for short spurts of hard work. They offer you a chance to boost your income a few times every year by pushing just a little harder.

The plan may have specific bonuses for your network reaching specific levels as well. These could be set cash amounts, larger commissions, or might be in the form of new cars, luxury trips, or free office supplies.

Another type of bonus is awarded for bringing in new distributors. The company might offer a $500 cash bonus for each distributor, but if you bring in five or more in a year you get an extra $1,000.

These plans are meant to motivate you. If you can make $900 in sales, they want you to be motivated to make $1,000. If the bonuses are fair, there are few drawbacks to these plans.

Forced Matrix Plans

Attempts to create a fairer situation for people who enter the network at a later stage of its development have resulted in forced matrix plans. In the simplest of these plans, you have an equal chance of ending up working for any distributor a level above you. In more complex plans, you actually could be put at the top of a network even though you are new to the business.

The objective of a forced matrix is to recruit a distributor for each available space in a predesigned organizational chart. When that is done, you form a new matrix—so instead of having a large, sprawling network, you can eventually have many individual little matrices. For example, if you're building a two-by-four matrix, there is a spot for you at the top, two underneath you, and two underneath each of those two people. As new distributors are recruited, they are assigned to a spot in the matrix. The further down the matrix you are, the less money you make from someone else's sale.

Forced matrix plans are very common in start-up companies because they are easier to control. Many organizations switch from forced matrix to unilevel plans as they age.

Although this is a simple example, these matrices can get very complex and sometimes require computer programs to place a person in the matrix. In unscrupulous companies, people are placed at low levels in the matrix and are told that the computer put them there.

One concern about this type of plan is how you can get out of your "box." Some plans allow you to start your own matrix once you reach a certain level of sales. Another variation is to require people to buy their way into a spot on the matrix. If you want to be at the top of the ladder, you pay more than if you want a spot at a lower level.

Another drawback is that you have no control over the placement of a new distributor. If you think someone would be exceptionally good, you can't place him or her underneath a good first-line person. They simply end up working for whomever the computer or other system says they should.

In spite of the drawbacks, forced matrix programs can work well, especially when the pool for distributors is fairly small and there will be a fair amount of actual selling going on. They tend to build a team atmosphere and, if people are allowed to break away and form their own matrices, there is ample incentive to continue selling and recruiting new distributors.

Plans with Legs

Many payment plans reward the person at the top of the network disproportionately to those underneath them. They are very popular because they can bring in quick money for the initial investors. Unfortunately, they also quickly fizzle because the new recruits learn that they have to work hard to make a fraction of the money they make for the people at the top. If you have a plan that limits the number of people at the top of a network, you have a "plan with legs."

Binary plans are probably the most common of this group, although there are trinary and other types as well. In a binary plan, you have only two people directly in your frontline (trinary would have three). Everyone else you recruit works underneath one of these two people.

These plans encourage people to work together by paying them for generating specific amounts of sales. A typical program will reward the two people at the top of the network when each of their "legs" makes a certain sales goal within a certain time period. For example, the plan might say that a commission of $100 is paid to each of the top people when each leg reaches at least $2,000 in sales revenue. The problem is that one leg may make $2,000 in revenue while the next might make $1,000. If that's the case, the top sponsor doesn't qualify for a commission.

Because binary and trinary plans offer the easiest way to make fast money, they also are used most often by illegal operations. Check the company and the compensation plan carefully to make sure it is legal.

These plans are the least stable, but they can provide a good solid income if the product line is diverse enough to support continual sales and if the plan offers reasonable opportunities for everyone to reach the top of a leg; some plans, for example, will put you at the top of a network when you personally reach a certain sales goal. More commonly, though, the plans are started by people who want to make quick money and then move on to another scheme.

Evaluating Your Compensation Plan

Compensation plans can be extremely confusing, especially if you are unfamiliar with network marketing. Your sponsor and other distributors will probably tell you that their compensation plan is the best there is, that you can become a millionaire in very little time, and that you won't have to work very hard at all.

No matter how well you know and like your potential sponsor, if you receive that message, the person is not telling you the whole truth. There is no easy way to make money, even in network marketing. If a plan promises big bucks early on, it is most likely a high-risk venture.

The Right Amount

No matter what business a company is in, it needs some money to pay its executives, buy or produce the product, pay bills generated by the home office, run marketing programs, and develop new products. Companies frequently put about 50 percent of their profits into operating costs and to reinvest in the company's growth. (This number may vary, as long as it's not less than 30 percent or more than 70 percent.)

To figure out if your company pays a reasonable amount to its distributors, tally up exactly how much could possibly be taken from one sale. Figure everyone's cut all the way down the line. If the company is giving more than 70 percent of every sale to its distributors, that's good news for today but could signal that it will run into trouble in the future, because it won't have the money to support expansion. If it gives less than 30 percent to its distributors, you have to question where the rest of that money is going.

Fairness to All Distributors

A program should offer everyone the opportunity to succeed, no matter where they enter the down-line. This can be a big problem with "legged" operations or with forced matrix plans because people are typically placed at a certain level and are moved to a different level only if they reach very high sales goals.

Step back and ask yourself how much you reasonably could sell in a month. Now divide that in half. (No matter how conservative we are, we have a tendency to be too optimistic about the sales, especially in the beginning.) What is your compensation on that half starting today? Does it seem fair for the amount of work you will be putting in?

 **SSENTIALS** No matter how confusing the compensation plan may appear, you should be able to figure it out completely. Run it by some friends or relatives to see if they can understand it. If they can't, the company might be trying to trick you.

Many companies give you a guaranteed percentage on sales that can be as high as 40 percent. This means that you receive $4 out of every $10 you make on a sale. It also means that an item that lists for $10 in your catalog really only costs you $6 if you buy it for personal use. This is especially important if you are working for a company that has a number of products you personally use. You may just find that you save enough on your own purchases to justify being a distributor.

You are the only person who can judge the fairness for the amount of work. If you really like to meet people and sell product and you hate your current job, making the equivalent of $6 an hour isn't too bad. If you're looking at this opportunity as a way to become financially independent, you will want to set your sights a little higher.

Ideally, you should expect to get at least $30 an hour for the time you put into the business right from the start. That means if you spend two hours at a sales party, your commission for the sales at that event should be at least $60.

The Down-Line Bonus

Most companies offer some type of incentive to recruit down-line members, although this can vary widely based on the company's marketing plan. Does the compensation plan seem fair? Obviously it takes more work to recruit someone than it does to make a sale. Do you get a bonus for all your hard work?

 You should receive some type of compensation for bringing in a new recruit. If you don't, make sure that you receive a large commission on your first-line recruit's sales. It should be no less than 5 percent lower than your commission on your own sales.

Some companies choose to give a nonmonetary reward for recruiting new distributors. The reward usually gets bigger with every distributor you recruit and often can be accumulated, like points, over the course of one or more years. For example, one company gives 100 points for every distributor you have recruited. They issue a catalog of luxury products such as computers, televisions, trips, and jewelry. The points can be saved up and used to "buy" those items.

Motivation Potential

The program should be motivating at all levels. Anyone entering at any point in the network should be encouraged to work hard. That's the biggest problem with a forced matrix program. Why should you be motivated to find a new distributor that goes into someone else's downline?

The standard compensation plan will be motivating if you see it as fair. However, you also want to look for extra motivation. Does the company offer an annual or quarterly contest where high sellers can earn trips, cars, or other luxury items? Are there bonuses when you reach certain levels, such as the Mary Kay pink Cadillac?

Take into account the amount of work you need to do to reach the next level of compensation. Are the steps short enough that it's easily reachable, at least in the beginning? Ask your potential sponsor how long it took him or her to attain the various levels in the program.

Also look for daily motivators that aren't part of the formal compensation plan. The company should respect its distributors and stay in contact with them, telling them of anything good or bad happening to the company. One study by a large consulting firm found that people found good communication with their superiors to be the biggest motivator in a job. The same is true in a network-marketing organization. You want to know at all times that the company is thriving and moving ahead.

Look for little things such as a newsletter for distributors, an annual gathering for all distributors, regional parties, and even motivational tactics such as letters from the home office when you do well or a supply of "You Can Do It" stickers to place on your bathroom mirrors. All of these belong to nonmonetary compensation category and are definitely important to your morale and long-term commitment.

Reasonable Expectations

The program shouldn't expect too much in terms of sales. Many companies encourage sales by setting the initial compensation very high, from 25 to 40 percent of the sale. This lets you see success right away.

Other companies don't pay much of anything until your sales reach a certain level, such as $1,000 a month. That can be motivating but also unrealistic and discouraging. Imagine putting in a great deal of work to learn the product and sales strategies only to get a few pennies from every sale. Sure, the company tells you that you can make big money after you hit various goals, but if you realistically can't reach these goals for several years, something is wrong with the goals.

Ask the company how many of their new distributors reach that goal within three months. Also ask how many quit before they ever reach it. Ask your sponsor how long it took him or her and how much work it took. The answers should give you a good indication of how reasonable the company's expectations are.

Volume Requirements

Some organizations require that you (and your down-line) purchase a certain amount of product every month. If you fail to meet that limit, you are penalized or even dropped from the ranks, often without being reimbursed for items that you might have purchased.

Sometimes that volume requirement is perfectly reasonable because it reflects the company's cost to help keep you in business. If, for example, you don't sell at least $50 a month, of which the company gets $25, it isn't worth the company's effort to keep you in the communications loop, supplied with updates on new products and marketing efforts. It is simply using the requirement as a way to weed out distributors who aren't really serious about the business.

The volume requirement should be reasonable for you to make in a bad month. Many companies set it at the amount a good, loyal customer might buy in a month. For example, if you sell nutritional supplements and the company has discovered that its best customers spend $100 a month, it's not unreasonable for them to set that as your volume requirement, because you should be able to spend that for your personal use.

Advantages for Newcomers

Some organizations offer advantages for the new distributors, giving them a few months of extra bonus money or bonuses for their first few down-line members. Some will even "seed" your prospect list by giving you a few customers from the person at the top of your up-line.

For example, one housewares network-marketing company gives its new distributors 35 percent commissions on their sales for the first three months (instead of the regular 25 percent) and an extra $200 (over and above the regular $400) for every new distributor they recruit during that time.

The idea is to have you see success right away so you are motivated to reach that level through hard work. There aren't too many disadvantages to such an option, except that you have to remember it will go away.

There is no magic to finding the right compensation program and the program shouldn't seem magical, either. If it seems as though it's extremely easy to make big money, you're likely missing something. If it seems like a lot of hard work, you have probably found a solid business opportunity.

The Realistic Middle Level

We'd all like to become millionaires, but what will you realistically make in the program? Find out what the typical distributor is making. How big is the typical down-line? If you work a forty-hour week, how much can you expect to be making after a year?

Be wary because most companies and sponsors like to tout the best examples. Remember to look realistically at your own situation—your sales knowledge and experience as well as the product's saturation in your geographic area—to determine how well you might do.

Ask to speak to other members of your sponsor's down-line. After all, they will be your peers, so you should have free rein to contact them whenever you want. Ask them how they are doing and how long it took to get there.

Then determine if you can live with that. After all, not everyone can become a millionaire, even if we work hard at it. Can you accept making the more realistic middle level of income?

What Is the Top?

Is there a cap on the program? It may seem far-fetched today, but if the program lets your distributors break away after they reach a certain level, you could see your retirement income fall away just because you hired some great distributors. Other programs stop giving you commission at a relatively early level in the down-line, such as the fourth generation. Still others begin compensating you with company stock instead of money long before you reach the million-dollar mark.

Don't trust the company's sales sheet. Ask to talk to people who have made it big. Is there a big supply of them? Are there new ones added to the group every year or is everyone an old-timer?

CHAPTER 8

Finding the Right Sponsor

F inding the right sponsor is a lot like finding the right spouse. Liking the person goes a long way, but the marriage will be stronger if you find someone who is willing to work for your success and complements your weak areas. When you are looking for a sponsor, you want to find a team player who knows how to lead and coach, not someone who sees you as a big dollar sign.

The Importance of a Good Sponsor

Your sponsor is your lifeline to the company. When you first begin working as a distributor, you will turn to your sponsor for everything from advice on making a sale to boosting your morale when you have a bad week. Your sponsor will know the people to call at the company when your paperwork is screwed up, your orders don't arrive on time, or you need extra training in a specific area.

ESSENTIALS

Your sponsor has a direct interest in your success. The products you sell and the new distributors you bring on board make your sponsor's paycheck bigger every month. Because of that, you should be able to demand a fair amount from this person.

Think of the relationship between you and your sponsor as a team effort. You are not your sponsor's employee or subordinate. You don't have to do exactly what the sponsor says, as if he or she were your boss, and you can expect the sponsor to share more information with you than many bosses would.

Look for Responsiveness

A good sponsor will be responsive to your needs. You can rely on your sponsor to answer any question you have within twenty-four hours, even if she works another full-time job, is traveling on business, or is on vacation. Likewise, if you say you're having trouble making cold calls, the sponsor should help you find the appropriate training or make some cold calls with you.

Responsiveness can be proactive as well. The sponsor should check in with you every few weeks to see how things are going. He should notice if your sales have fallen, if you're having trouble selling a new category, or if all your pitches to potential distributors seem to fail. In these situations—and many more—the sponsor should give personal advice or recommend training materials long before you have to ask for it.

Look for Respect

You should trust your sponsor to respect you, treat you as a professional, and guide you into new areas. The sponsor shouldn't make you feel dumb, no matter how basic your questions may be, and has no right to be patronizing.

Respect comes in many forms. First, the sponsor should respect your reasons for getting into network marketing. For example, if you never intend to pursue this as a full-time career, the sponsor shouldn't try to convince you to change your mind. Likewise, if you prefer to sell products and not concentrate too much on attracting additional distributors into your down-line, that also is a decision your sponsor should respect.

Respect is the most important ingredient in your relationship with your sponsor. If your sponsor doesn't respect you, he or she will be unable to provide you with the advice and tools you need to succeed.

The sponsor should also respect the way you do business. Hopefully, your sponsor has had a fair amount of success in her network-marketing business, and you should learn from that success, but that doesn't mean you have to do everything exactly the same way this person did. If you prefer a soft sell over a hard sell, the choice should be left up to you.

Look for Mentoring Ability

The best sponsors are not just good at network marketing, they know how to teach other people to be good at it, too. Chances are, you have met many people in your life who were excellent at something—knitting, hunting, dog training, swimming, or whatever—but could never teach their skills to anybody. The fact is, things come so naturally to some people that they just can't explain how to do it.

If that's the case with your potential sponsor, you could be in trouble. There is nothing more frustrating than someone who says "Just do it" when you mention that you're having trouble in a specific area.

Instead, you want someone who can patiently take you through every step of the process. You want someone who remembers exactly how he did something and can tell you just how to do it.

A good mentor has the ability to give you the right information even before you need it. She tells you what the next step will be and what her personal plans are for the business. If she hears about a new product line coming out, that information should be passed on to you as soon as possible.

FACTS

A good mentor is both a friend and an advisor. She will tell you when you are doing something wrong and suggest a solution. She also will praise you lavishly when you do something right.

The best mentors know how to give a gentle push and some encouragement toward success. Your sponsor should constantly tell you that he knows you can do better because you have it in you.

A good mentor also knows how to motivate you. If you're having a bad week, the mentor knows if you need a pep talk, a new goal, a "me too" chat, or some additional training. She should know whether you like difficult goals or find them too intimidating, whether you like to be praised in public or find it embarrassing, and whether you can take honest criticism well or whether it needs to be softened a bit.

Friendship Is Not the Best Policy

Never mix business with pleasure. That's an old saying, but it's very true in network marketing. Many a friendship (or even a family relationship) has been ruined because the sponsor had too many expectations of his distributors, who were family and friends.

Good friends and family members can be risky sponsors simply because they like you. They might have difficulty telling you the truth because they are afraid of the repercussions. Could your younger brother really tell you that you need some heavy-duty sales training or that you don't understand the product well enough yet?

Friends and family might trust you too much. They may assume that because you are a friend or relative, you will work hard for them no matter what. As a result, they won't work to motivate you and they might give you far less attention than they would someone else.

Friends and family members frequently fail as good sponsors because your relationship is too close. Proceed carefully. Choose a good friend or family member as your sponsor only if you are sure that you can build a business relationship in addition to your personal one.

No Pity Allowed

Some people choose a family member or good friend because they feel sorry for the person and want to help them out. After all, you're planning to enter into a network-marketing opportunity anyway, so why not give Uncle George the benefit of your work?

Look at it from a business perspective. If Uncle George needs your pity, he likely wouldn't be a very good sponsor, would he?

Rules Are Meant to Be Broken

Of course, there are exceptions to every rule. There are some friends and family members that make excellent sponsors. The key is to examine your reasons carefully and be honest with yourself.

If your friend or relative is a true business leader who will respect you as a person and let you run the business the way you want, you could end up having a great working relationship. Not only will you be getting the support you need, but every sale you make will be helping a good friend or family member, too.

Looking at the Track Record

The best predictor of a person's value as a sponsor is how well she does with her own network-marketing business. You will want to examine everything from how long it took your sponsor to build a good down-line to how much product she sells every month.

Don't be shy when you ask about your sponsor's track record. Unless you are a natural salesperson, you will be modeling many of your sales strategies and tactics on his or her successes. It's important that your sponsor is successful and understands the reasons behind that success.

At the same time, a good track record is not enough. Remember that you are entering the business at a different point. Your sponsor may have been successful in the past, when the product line was still unique—before the competition really took off. Would the sponsor have been as successful in the current tougher market?

FACTS

A good sponsor will have a well-balanced business resume. You want to see just enough failure to know the person can empathize with you and has had an opportunity to learn from his or her mistakes. Too much success can make a person cocky and unsympathetic.

Pay Attention to Your Sponsor's Down-Line

Before you choose your sponsor, you want to look at his down-line. Ideally, the sponsor should already be working with at least three or four other people. However, everyone has to start somewhere, so you could end up being the first in someone's down-line. Although that situation is riskier than entering a thriving down-line, it can also be exciting because you can work as a team to build the business.

Assuming there are others in the down-line, ask to talk to two or three of them. Are they happy? What does the sponsor do to support them? Would they like more support? Is the motivation good? Do they feel pushed and cajoled, or do they feel they are given adequate respect when trying to reach a goal? Does the sponsor communicate her expectations?

Failures Are Okay

When Lee Iacocca was hired by Chrysler in 1978 to turn around the company's business, the board of directors were impressed that he had been in charge of the failed Edsel division. Why? Because they reasoned that since he had made his share of mistakes, he would also know how to avoid them.

Believe it or not, you want a sponsor who has had a bit of adversity in this business. If everything went great for the sponsor, he won't be able to relate to your problems and will expect you to do just as well as he did.

Success Counts

While a bit of failure is good for any businessperson, you also want to see some successes. You want to be assured that this person knows how to succeed in network marketing so that she can pass those skills on to you.

In terms of recruiting new distributors, look for someone who has not only recruited a large down-line fairly quickly but whose down-line has stayed in business—that means your sponsor understands how to sell the business to others, as well as how to keep a down-line motivated.

In terms of selling the product, look for someone who makes at least 10 percent of her income from direct sales. You want to make sure that this person is staying with the business, believes in the product, and has experience meeting new sales challenges as they arise.

Ask the Right Questions

Some network marketers are excellent at developing a sales pitch you can't say no to. They lay out everything so perfectly and it all sounds so wonderful that you're ready to sign the papers—and the associated check—before you even think about it.

If that urge strikes you, it's time to step back and suggest a formal interview with the prospective sponsor, even if he is a good friend or family member. You want to make sure that the person is sincere about helping you succeed, not just when he is making a formal presentation to you.

Suggest a neutral spot such as a local café so that you can ask questions without being distracted. Bring a notebook and write one of the following questions at the top of each page. Also add any additional questions you might have about the products or the company. Don't leave the table until you have an answer to every question!

Why Do You Want Me to Join?

If your sponsor wants you as part of her down-line in order to get a bonus or make more money, that's okay, but there should also be other reasons. Look for answers such as, "Because I think you'd be great at this. You like people and you love the product. I'd like to see you get out of that dead-end job and do something that you can be proud of."

Again, try to judge the person's sincerity. Avoid sponsors who seem to spout company lines such as "This is the opportunity of a lifetime."

Continue to ask questions until you get to the heart of the prospective sponsor. Don't accept prepared answers. Look for someone who thinks carefully before responding to your questions.

How Much Do You Want to Grow in This Business?

A good answer is that the person views this as a job and knows that there is room for growth. Be wary of people who say they want to become millionaires and then retire (and live off your hard work).

Look for realistic expectations here. If you have done your research on the product and have found that it has a relatively small niche in the marketplace, be wary of someone who says they want their first-generation down-line to have 100 people by the end of the year.

In fact, a good sponsor may actually say that they don't want their first-generation down-line to get too big because they want to spend their time finding quality people and helping them build quality businesses.

How Much Work Will I Need to Put In?

That's a good question to ask when trying to gauge how much the potential sponsor is thinking of you. You want someone who is flexible enough to understand that you might not want to jump in full-time right away.

The best answer is that you should set a reasonable financial goal every year and work toward it. If the prospective sponsor starts talking about full-time work and the wonderful income potential, and you're not yet ready for that leap, ask exactly how little you can do to still be considered successful.

One excellent sponsor for a home-products network-marketing company tells her prospective recruits that they should plan to sell $300 of product a month and recruit three people into their down-line in the first year. With that company's compensation plan, that gives the person $75 a month plus an extra $450 in new-recruit bonuses. It's enough to make a difference in paying bills, she reasons. Any less than that, she explains to the recruits, will soon get discouraging because you don't see any real benefit to the work you do.

What Is Your Mission?

Good sponsors will have missions that go beyond money. Sure, they may want to become millionaires and retire early, but they should also say that they like to be self-employed, that they like to work with people, that they believe in this product, and that when it comes to being a sponsor, they want to "help people be all they can be."

One sponsor for a natural health products company always tells her recruits about the housewife who couldn't drive a car and was so shy she wouldn't even go to a church group meeting. The sponsor worked with the woman, and she now travels across the country speaking at company meetings, telling other people how being in network marketing can literally change your life.

Why Did You Get into This Business?

Look for honesty and sincerity in this response. If you get an answer that sounds rehearsed, rephrase the question. Go beyond the first answer and try to figure out the real reasons. If a potential sponsor says she wanted to be self-employed, find out if she was looking for a way to supplement the family's income while being able to stay home.

Don't pry into the sponsor's personal life. What you want to know is what motivates your potential sponsor. Even if you have nothing in common with your sponsor, you will have a better sense of how this person judges success and what he or she wants out of life.

How Can You Help Me Succeed?

Many a prospective sponsor will be taken aback by this question. In response, they might mention all the support the company offers and may make vague references to their experience. While these people aren't necessarily bad sponsors, there are others who could do better.

If you find a prospective sponsor who responds by saying that he will spend at least one day a month with you for the first three months helping you learn the products and the company while also helping you make sales calls, you know you've found a very good sponsor.

Similarly, if a prospective sponsor tells you that she personally produces a little one-page newsletter that reviews successes people have had with difficult customers or entering new markets and distributes this newsletter to her down-line, you are in good shape. Many good sponsors will also talk about meetings they hold for everyone in their down-line and how they encourage the sharing of sales strategies among their down-line.

Means of Communication

Now that you have asked your questions and gotten some responses, you might begin to get a better idea of your prospective sponsor's communication style. Communication is a key component in any business relationship. As a down-line member, you want to know what is going on with your sponsor. Has he or she recruited any new distributors? Has there been success in recent sales? Is there any more information that can be passed along? Are there any sales secrets to be shared?

You also need to know what is happening at the company. While the company will most likely communicate directly with you on major issues, your sponsor has been around longer than you and may be plugged into events you aren't aware of.

The Control Freak

Before you even make your decision to get involved, this person calls you every day to see if you are signing on today. This is a sign that he or she will be too controlling. Chances are, this sponsor won't let you run your business the way you want, will nag you to attend meetings, and will constantly call to find out how much you have sold.

You can't get away from a control freak. These people believe that success is in the details and the details need to be managed. For them, it's always worked well, but if this is a personality you can't work with, you'd best look for a different sponsor.

On the other hand, if you are extremely nervous about the opportunity, a control freak can help by taking you through the first few months step by step. Hopefully, by the time you are comfortable with the business, the sponsor will have found a new recruit to control.

SSENTIALS Evaluate your likes and dislikes in communication styles before you decide if you can work with an extreme personality. If you are leaving your current job because your boss is a control freak, you probably don't want a control freak for a sponsor.

The Ghost

You thought you had a good relationship. You said you were interested, but you haven't heard from the sponsor in weeks. Will this person leave you hanging once you've signed on, too?

Ghosts are frightening sponsors because you never know what is happening with them. Sometimes they will quit the business and even leave the state without bothering to tell you. That may be fine if you're well into developing your own business, but if you're in the beginning stages, having a ghost for a sponsor can spell the end of your business before it ever gets off the ground.

Even in the best circumstances—where you know what you're doing and how to do it—having a ghost for a sponsor is frustrating because you are very aware that this person is making money off your hard work, yet giving you nothing in return.

The Blob

You're nervous. You just don't know if this is right. You tell the potential sponsor about your concerns, and in response you get a shrug and something like "it's up to you"—and that's that.

It's clear that you cannot rely on a sponsor like that for help. The blob doesn't disappear, like a ghost, but he or she won't really do anything to help you. If you ask a question, the response will likely be "I don't know" or "Call me if you find the answer, because that's a good question."

For some reason, family members and good friends are the most common blobs. Perhaps it's because they are afraid of giving you advice.

The Pressure Cooker

The sponsor insists you sign on, says you're being foolish for worrying, and says she can't understand why you would let this opportunity pass by you. In fact, if you don't sign on today, the sponsor threatens, this opportunity will go to someone else.

Whoa. That sounds like a disaster just waiting to happen. After all the pressure of signing up before you are sure that you are ready, you are likely to find yourself with a sponsor who suddenly turns into a ghost or a blob. The reason is that this type of sponsor enjoys the chase—once you are captured, the game is over and the sponsor moves on to the next victim.

Or, the pressure-cooker attitude won't change. Like the control freak, this person will call you constantly, but not just to check on your numbers. The pressure cooker will always make it sound like this month's goals are a matter of life and death.

Some pressure cookers are actually fun to work with because they show a great deal of energy and have many ideas to offer. If you can deal with the constant stress these people exude and keep your own goals in mind, this may work for you.

How can I tell if my pressure-cooker sponsor will cool down after I sign on?
The best way to find out is to ask other members of this person's down-line. If that isn't possible, ask your prospective sponsor how he or she envisions your relationship in three months, six months, or a year.

The Sponsor's Sponsor

Remember that you are not just signing up to be a member of your sponsor's down-line. You are part of the down-line of everyone above your sponsor as well. Realistically, you should be able to count the people at least three steps above your sponsor as part of your own up-line.

Note that much of the support you get will be modeled on the support your own sponsor receives from his or her up-line. You should be invited to meetings sponsored by your up-line and receive written communications they offer. Likewise, if you have any questions about the business, you should be free to call these people for help.

Your sponsor's sponsor is especially important if your prospective sponsor is relatively new in the business. If you are one of his or her first recruits, you want to know that you will be taken care of by someone with a little more experience. In fact, you may want to interview this person as closely as you do the prospective sponsor.

Even more important, these people can help you determine if your prospective sponsor is a good fit for you. Ask about your prospective sponsor's communication style. Find out what your prospective sponsor's strengths and weaknesses are.

No matter what your final decision regarding a sponsor, remember that you have many people in your up-line to help you. Be sure they are willing to help, then use them wisely.

FACTS

Your sponsor's sponsor is the best indicator of the type of support you will receive from your own sponsor. Look for someone "higher up" who is still involved in the business and offers good advice to your sponsor without being too controlling.

CHAPTER 9

Company-Sponsored Training

You have chosen your product, your network-marketing company, and your sponsor. Now what? You are excited about getting started, but you just don't have a grasp on everything there is to know about the items you need to sell and all the tools that are available to help you. Your company should be able to either offer you advice on everything from sales strategies to building a Web site or refer you to someone who can help.

Product Training

Selling even the most basic products requires some type of training. You need to be able to answer your own, your customers', and your prospective down-line members' questions about such basic things as where the item was made and what it is made out of.

For example, you're selling a line of candles. That's great. We know that they provide light and probably a bit of fragrance. But what is different about these candles? Are they made of paraffin, beeswax, palm oil, or something else? Are the colors and fragrances natural or synthetic? Are they handmade or mass-produced? How long do they last? Are they poisonous to dogs, cats, and toddlers? Will they melt in the trunk of a car in the summer or crumble apart in cold weather?

You can ask these questions—and more—about a particular candle. But what about a whole line of various candles and candle holders? Suddenly, the simple little product line you thought you could easily handle seems very complex.

SSENTIALS

In virtually every circumstance, the company should provide a book of product information that answers any question you or a prospect could possibly have about the item.

What Is the Product?

The first question to be answered is what the product is and what it is meant to do. That can seem silly—everyone knows a candle is meant to provide a little heat, a little light, and possibly a little fragrance—but some things can surprise you. For example, a popular line of candles shaped like figurines is actually made for strictly decorative purposes. Sure, you can burn them, but they are really meant to be displayed as you would a statuette.

Likewise, candles can have other purposes. Some are meant to keep insects away. Some add ambience to a romantic setting. Some have strong scents meant to mask odors. Some are used to heat food. Some are infused with fragrances that help people sleep, relieve sinus problems, or even improve a person's mood.

How Is It Made?

You also need to know how the item is manufactured and what it is made out of. You should know exactly what your products are made out of, because in today's marketplace people often want to know if products are recyclable and have natural ingredients.

The way the product is made can have a major impact, too. Let's look at another item—black pepper. The Watkins Company sells pepper that it says does not make people sneeze. It really doesn't. That's because this pepper is cracked instead of ground.

FACTS

Any product is as complex as you want it to be. If you feel your prospects will want to know the chemical formula for the composite in the bottle your product comes in, push until you get the answer.

Let's say you've decided to sell home-decorating products. You know what they are made of and, frankly, how they're made really isn't a big deal to your customers because it's pretty apparent they're made in a factory. Ah, but where is that factory? If it's in a third-world country, are the people paid well, do they work in safe conditions, and does the factory follow U.N. guidelines on child labor laws?

You may find that your products are handmade by indigenous laborers using local ingredients. Or perhaps the ingredients are gathered by locals and the item is made in the United States, as is frequently the case with herbal remedies. Those are facts you should know because they could entice some people to choose your products over your competitor's.

What about the Company?

A part of product training is learning more about the company. How was it founded? What is its history? What are its best-selling items? Why does it sell through direct sales?

These kinds of questions relate to product training for two reasons. First, when people purchase your products, they are also buying the items' brand name, so you want to know what stands behind that name. Second, the company is the product that you sell to prospective down-line members.

Sales Training

You can't expect to read a few things about the products and then go out and sell them. The whole art of selling requires a number of skills and a fair amount of practice. Sure, some people seem to be natural salespeople, but they are the people who learn the skills more quickly than the rest of us.

For the most part, sales training should include a look at each item and what makes it better than a competing product. The training should also examine how to sell these products to different personality types.

ESSENTIALS

Throughout sales training, remember that you have two product lines. The first encompasses all the items you will be selling directly to consumers. The second is the network-marketing opportunity you will be selling to potential distributors.

Sales training takes many forms. A good company will offer several opportunities for sales training, including one-on-one coaching, written materials, and ongoing help.

In-House Training

Ideally, the company will bring you into the office for at least a day to learn the basics of sales. Often these sessions are optional, but they are highly recommended because you get a sense of how the company likes its products to be sold.

When you attend these sessions, the trainers will expect you to have browsed through the product materials so you know what the products are and how they differ from similar items people can buy in stores. You will focus on these points when making a sale.

During the in-house training you should hear from at least one person who has done an excellent job as a distributor—the sales trainer or another person brought in just for an hour or two to answer your questions.

This "real-life" expert should focus on the reality of selling the product. He or she may even tell you that one of the strategies the trainer told you about doesn't really work very well and should be able to teach you little "tricks of the trade" that convince people to buy.

QUESTIONS?

What if the company doesn't offer any sales training beyond the most basic?
There are many sales-training organizations that offer public seminars that start at under $100 a day. Ask your local chamber of Commerce what is planned for your area.

The in-house training should give you a chance to practice selling in a small group, especially if you are new to the company. You should have a chance to use some basic strategies for making a cold call and over-coming common objections such as "I don't have time" or "I'm broke."

Expert Material

Whether you attend in-house sales training or not, the company should provide you with a sales manual that suggests how to sell the products as well as the direct-marketing opportunity. (You should refer to your sales manual and your product manual before virtually every sales call, because they are the cornerstones of your sales effort.)

The sales manual should include all of the information on the product benefits and ways to present that benefit to different people. It may not necessarily tell you about the different personality types (Chapter 15 in this book can help with that), but it should give you at least two reasons each product characteristic could be a benefit to someone.

The manual should also present a style of selling. Many companies contract with a popular sales consultant to present his or her methods for landing a sale and getting repeat business. Whether the method is well-known is not as important as the fact that there is a method that takes you through the various stages of a sale and gives advice on how to overcome common objections. This should be presented at a very basic level so that someone who has never talked in front of a group or who has never tried to sell something knows exactly what to do.

The manual should also provide some basic sales scripts to walk you through the most common sales situations. These include the cold call, the sales party, and selling a new item.

Ongoing Sales Training

In addition to the sales training you receive when you first join the company as a distributor, the company should provide periodic sales-training updates via a newsletter, e-mail, or audiotape. In addition, your sponsor may provide periodic sales information via photocopied articles from sales magazines or even a newsletter containing his or her own ideas.

Advanced sales skills can cover everything from working with different personality types to handling complex objections from people you are trying to sell on becoming part of your down-line. Some people are more ready for this information than others, so it is usually presented as optional information in a format that can be stored for future reference.

If the company says its product can be sold to anyone, find some outside sales training. No product can possibly meet the needs of everyone at every stage in life.

Sales Coaching

Your most important sales coach should be your sponsor. She has a direct interest in your success and should be there to work with you whenever you want. You can expect your sponsor to help you with difficult sales, especially when working to recruit a new distributor. The sponsor should be able to give you advice on how to proceed and what has worked for her in similar situations. The sponsor also should be able to tell you some of her tricks of the trade and constantly coach you on how to better "read" what a prospect might be interested in.

However, a good network-marketing company will also have in-house sales coaches. These are often the sales trainers or perhaps people who have done so well as distributors that they are paid a salary to spread their expertise. You should be able to call these people with any question, no matter how basic it might seem.

Marketing Support

Marketing is the part of the business that helps tell prospective customers about the products and the company. It can range from national advertising on television and in magazines to such simple tools as a chart that compares the product to its competition. The important thing is that the company provides you with some information to help you make the sale.

The basic marketing support is a product catalog, brochure, or folder. These should be supplied to you at a reasonable cost, because you will be giving or mailing them to many people during your sales efforts. Some companies will provide just one copy of the product catalog printed off the computer and expect you to photocopy it or print more yourself.

While a high-quality, printed catalog usually tells your customers that the product is viable and the company is legitimate, it's also very important that the catalog fits the company. For example, if you are selling all-natural nutritional items from the rainforest, you might want to see a catalog printed with soy ink on recyclable paper. A company selling high-end home decorating items should have high-quality brochures. A new company with just a few items could get by with the computer-printed version.

Sales Brochures

Many companies have periodic sales based on the season of the year, to introduce new products, or to liquidate items they will no longer carry. These sales brochures tend to run smaller than the main catalog and can be used to stay in touch with past customers. The sales usually last only a month or two, so mailing the brochure gives you a good excuse to follow up with a phone call.

Like the product catalog, the brochure should fit the company and the sale. Most important, however, is the fact that it should be inexpensive for you to buy in large quantities since you will want to send them to everyone on your current, past, and prospective customer list.

Miscellaneous Support

Many companies offer signage that can be placed in your car or on your front lawn. These are excellent tools if you have a well-known product that people recognize by name.

Advertising novelties such as key chains and pencils are good tools if you do mostly sales parties. They also work well for county fairs or as little gifts for the holidays.

Clothing is another fun way to advertise that you are in business. Many companies will offer T-shirts, denim shirts, caps, and scarves with their logos on them. You can wear them yourself, use them as gifts for good customers, and offer them as prizes at sales parties.

Some companies encourage their distributors to work fairs and even rent space at shopping malls. To help with these strategies, they will likely have signage and possibly even complete displays that you can purchase or rent.

Many companies suggest that their distributors put ads in small-town newspapers. In this case, they should provide a sample of the copy and possibly even some black-and-white logos that can be used in the advertisement.

Just because it's available doesn't mean you need it. Start with the essential marketing tools and add others, such as key chains or press releases, as your business grows and you find you really need them.

Public relations pieces such as a standard press release that discusses your involvement in a local charity activity or the fact that you have won an award are a subtle but useful marketing tool. The company should have a sample that you can simply rewrite, filling in the important information about yourself, and send to the local newspapers and radio stations.

Basic Business Supplies

As you will quickly find out, a home-based business needs many types of supplies. Some of these—product order sheets and marketing materials—can be obtained only from your network-marketing company. You might have to pay for these items, but the cost should be minimal.

Your company may also offer you computer software to use in the business. If it is mandatory, such as a customized ordering software program designed just for that company, it should be included in any initial fees you incur when you become a distributor.

FACTS

A good salesperson knows that the more exposure a product receives, the easier it will be to sell. Many companies offer supplies such as customized stationery, business cards, Post-It notes, calendars, and refrigerator magnets with their name and logo for use in your business correspondence.

Other basic business supplies that might be supplied by the company are customized materials such as business cards and letterhead. When a company supplies these, it usually does so at a large discount to you because the company uses an in-house print shop or contracts with a print shop to do a large order at once.

If the company doesn't supply these, it likely supplies the materials you need to create your own customized materials. This might include a CD with the company logo or preprinted logos. The company might also provide the specs that tell you what typeface you can use to create your materials.

Some network-marketing companies are so large that they are able to provide discounts on virtually every office supply you might need, from furniture and computers to folders and staplers. Furthermore, buying from the company will save you the time it takes to shop for everything you need.

Business Advice

In addition to giving you information about the products and how to sell them, the company should help you in starting your own business. It should have people or written materials that provide information on virtually every part of running your business.

Ideally, the company will have information available on any legal topic that could come up, such as how to hire family members or what to do if a competitor says you have defamed his business. Most importantly, you should receive information on liability and accounting laws.

Another area the company should provide information on is how to set up and run a business. Look for information on everything from how to set up your filing system to choosing the right insurance. Other topics you should have access to include how to write business letters, how to market the business, how to manage your time, and how to deal with the frustrations of being self-employed.

SSENTIALS

If the company doesn't have in-house expertise in a certain area such as small-business law, it should have a list of people or Web sites who can give you free advice on general questions. It also should have a lawyer on retainer for more difficult questions.

This material can come in a number of different formats. Some companies provide a newsletter with tips in all these areas. Others simply refer you to an internal expert if you call with a question. The important thing is that the company doesn't leave you isolated when you have concerns about the business. You want to know that the company cares enough to help you make it through your challenges.

Online Resources

There is no question that the Internet is a valuable resource for business, and that is especially true in the field of network marketing. An e-mail account will let you communicate with customers, with your company, and with other distributors.

The company Web site will help you market your products. E-mail will help you spread your messages and allow you to avoid cold calling. At the same time, internal sites or "intranets" can be used to conduct a lot of business that used to happen through the mail.

Public Web Sites

In today's marketplace, the network-marketing company that doesn't have a good Web site is destined for failure. Many customers like to check out the company's Web site before they order products from it, and many people looking for network-marketing opportunities will judge the potential of a company by its public Web site.

The home page should introduce the visitor to the company and its products. It should tell you how long the company has been in business, what its mission is, and what basic product lines it offers. It should also include a phone number and street address so people can call or write to the company for more information. (If this information is not provided, people can become very suspicious—and with good reason: Why would a legitimate company hide its address and phone number from the public?) The Web site should also have links to pages that deal with particular product lines.

When looking at the company's Web site, make sure the information is updated frequently. There is nothing more suspicious to a prospect than a Web site that appears to be a year or more out of date.

Another link should take people to a page that discusses the benefits of becoming a distributor for the company. Although the information need not be very specific, there should be a phone number for those who are interested in learning the details. Ideally, this page will also link to a few stories of distributors who were successful in working with the company.

A good Web site will also provide a list of distributors from whom the Web site visitor can purchase the products. You don't want a company that sells directly over the Web, taking business away from distributors like you.

Personal Web Sites

At the same time, many larger network-marketing companies are starting to see the value in setting up individual Web sites for their direct-sales representatives. Existing customers can visit these sites and order directly from them. You are credited with the order just as if you took it manually.

These sites are usually set up as templates with small portions that you can customize (insert your picture and a message from you to your customers). Sometimes you have the option of highlighting specific items or providing information such as tips for using the products. For example, food companies might encourage you to include recipes or meal planners.

Take a good look at your prospect list before you decide to sign up for a personal Web site. Do most of your prospects own computers? Do they like to make purchases online? You won't change their habits just because you now have a Web site.

While a personal Web site may cost a couple hundred dollars to set up and will take several hours a month to maintain, it serves as an excellent tool for a growing business. You receive your own Web site address and your good customers simply go there every week or month to see what's on sale or what's new about the product. They can also refer their friends to your site instead of hosting a sales party.

These sites aren't as valuable if your company has a small product line or a one-time-sale item. If that's the case, it makes more sense to have just one company-sponsored Web site that refers newcomers to distributors based on geography.

Intranet and E-mail Accounts

Your network-marketing company might also have an internal Web site that is set up for distributors who need to do business with the company. Typically, such a site will allow you to place your orders online instead of mailing them in, check on the status of an order, and even check inventory. You may also use it to receive company announcements, sales training information, or to chat with other distributors.

If the company doesn't have an internal Web site or network—and most smaller companies still don't—you should at least have an e-mail directory of the people who work for your company, in case you need to contact them.

Although we live in the age of computers, remember that these services are still time-consuming and expensive. A large company that has been around for several decades may have many Internet options, while a start-up company barely has a Web site. Don't be discouraged if your company is just beginning to develop its presence on the Web, but do encourage them along the way.

CHAPTER 10

The First Order of Business

This chapter will outline the first steps you will need to take to prepare yourself for your new job, from finalizing your start-up plan to figuring out the best way of telling your friends and family about your decision. Take care with every one of these steps so that your new career will begin on the right foot.

Choosing a Start-Up Plan

Most companies will offer several start-up options that require various degrees of financial input on your part. Some plans can start as low as just $20, but it's more typical to need to invest at least $100 to start up as a distributor, and some organizations even require a minimum of $500.

Don't let a high start-up cost scare you, though. First, it's a way the company can make sure you are serious about working the business. It's not uncommon for a company that has a low-end start-up plan to find that people join as distributors as a way to buy the product for themselves and have no intention of selling it to others or of finding other distributors. If you have a bigger investment to recoup, you're more likely to really work the business.

At the same time, the start-up kits are usually worth a good deal. Furthermore, the more money you put in, the more sample products you receive. Most companies encourage you to use those sample items so that you will be truly enthusiastic about them.

Higher start-up costs usually point to more services that the company provides for you, such as four-color product catalogs and even a personal Web site. You may find that the cost of buying these services later in your relationship with the company far exceeds the cost of getting them in the beginning because you can no longer take advantage of the discount packages offered to new recruits.

What Can You Afford?

While the frills are nice, they aren't absolutely necessary to start a thriving network-marketing business. You know that if you have to, you can get by with just a few brochures and a few sample products.

How much can you realistically invest for a start-up plan? If you are a poor college student or a struggling newlywed, you probably don't want to go with the high-end package. You just want a small sampling of the products and a few product catalogs—after all, most of your customers will be people like you, so they will understand your limited item selection and the fact that they have to share catalogs.

One thing to look for is a company that will let you pick and choose your original sample products instead of providing you with a standard kit. For example, if you are a college student and you are becoming a distributor for a vitamin and mineral supplement company, you would probably prefer the products geared for younger people than those for the elderly.

Assume that you will never again see the money you spend on your start-up kit and you will know exactly how much to spend. Consider this a luxury purchase, and you will suddenly find that you can do without many of the frills.

If you are going to be working for a home-decorating business, consider your typical customers. If country-style decorating is big in your part of the country, you likely won't want the French Provençal stuff.

Do Your Potential Customers Know the Product?

If the product has a good reputation, you probably don't need more than the bare bones and a few extra catalogs. Chances are, your customers will even tell you about some of the items that are available.

You can judge this when you begin to talk to people about starting the business. Do they say, "Oh, yeah, I love their products," or do they say, "I've never heard of them. What do they carry?"

You can also judge this from your own instincts. If you have heard of the products before and have used them for a few years, it is likely that others in your peer group have heard of them, too.

If the product line is new, you should probably spend more money on a start-up kit. You will need to advertise the fact that you are in business and you will need to educate your customers about the variety and the benefits of your products.

Now, this isn't to say that you shouldn't align yourself with a new company. Some of the best opportunities in network marketing are available when the company is newer and you can get in on the ground floor. Just remember that the less well-known the company products are, the more marketing materials you will need to help your customers gain that familiarity.

Will You Use the Products?

A number of companies actually encourage you to use the products and even take your well-worn items to sales parties to show that you use the products yourself and for the purpose of demonstrating how the worn items hold up. In such cases, it's to your advantage to buy the items you know you will use. You will get the items you want for yourself at a discount, and before you know it, they will be helping you to increase your sales.

If you don't plan to use the products, however, there is no reason to purchase them for yourself. For example, if you're selling Tupperware containers, you probably don't need them in all of the different sizes that are available. Your customers will understand that because you have six children, you chose the big containers, but they can get by with the smaller versions.

Do You Need the Marketing Materials?

Often the higher-end "kits" will include such things as free customized Web sites, marketing materials such as magnetic signs for your cars, testimonial videos, or software to put the company's logo on your letterhead.

These items can be well worth the money, but only if you decide to use them. If you decide to go with a higher-end introductory package because it offers you a Web site but you don't update the site at least monthly, you've wasted the money. If you get the letterhead stationery but never write a single letter, the stationery will do you no good.

Before you commit to a package that has all these frills, consider each item carefully and determine if you will really use it and if using it will help you in your business. For example, let's say you decide to get the magnetic signs for your car but then you discover that your major customer base is right in your neighborhood and word-of-mouth has people knocking at your door asking for the products. The signs didn't give you much new business, so they weren't worth the money.

Let's say the package you're considering has a nice testimonial video to help you gain new recruits. The problem is that you can't imagine showing a video to any of your friends right now or even asking them to take it home. If you can't imagine how you would use it, you probably won't, at least in the beginning.

Be wary of companies that ask you to invest thousands of dollars in becoming a distributor. You should be able to set up your entire business, from start-up kit through office essentials, with less than $3,000, although you may choose to spend more.

Can You Earn the Kit?

Some organizations will let you earn the money for your start-up kit by selling products for a month or two and getting the same commission as if you had already signed on. You usually have to make the commitment that you will become a distributor, but you don't have to decide which start-up kit to buy until later in the process.

In this case, you usually rely on your sponsor to supply the marketing materials during that time. Consequently, before you go this route, be sure your sponsor is willing to help you out to this extent. Chances are, you will find out about this option from him or her so it won't be a problem, but it's best to ask.

Other organizations ask you to commit to a specific start-up kit but don't make you pay for it for two or three months, letting you use your first commissions toward the price. The problem with this option is that you might decide to go with a bigger kit than you really need and find that sales don't come as quickly as you had hoped. You could get stuck paying hundreds of dollars for items you can't possibly use yourself.

Can You Make the Marketing Materials Yourself?

There is no substitute for having the real products on hand when you're trying to sell them, but you can frequently get by with a small sampling if you have marketing materials that show the rest of the products.

Often a network-marketing company will let you download pictures from their Internet site to create your own product catalogs. This lets you pick and choose what you think your typical customers might be interested in while also saving you the cost of buying professionally printed brochures. Of course, you will still have the cost of printing the brochures on your own computer. You also might have to pay the company a small fee for using the photos.

Do not photocopy or download images from the Internet unless you have permission to do so from the company. You could be violating several different laws, including trademarks and copyrights.

Other materials don't have to include photos. You can create your own price lists, newsletters, and testimonial sheets (stories of happy customers) without a lot of work. However, unless you are a whiz at the computer, the materials will definitely not be as nice as those provided by the company. That can be a disadvantage if you're trying to make a professional presentation.

How Much to Invest in the Business

The best way to determine how much to invest in this business as a whole is to look at what you hope to gain from it. As difficult as it is, you will have to decide now how much effort you will be putting into this business in the next three years.

For example, if you're a housewife looking for a little extra spending money every month, you won't want to spend more than $1,000 to get set up. You might even decide you won't spend more than $100.

Whatever your decision, remember that you can always increase your investment at a later date, so there is no need to overspend.

Think of the business as a lifestyle tradeoff for a year. For example, you might want to forego one nice meal out every week for a year and use that money to start the business. You might also decide to sell that vintage car sitting in your garage or those antique books taking up shelf space in your den.

FACTS

A good rule of thumb is to look at what you realistically think you can make in one year. Now cut that in half. Take 10 percent of that half and use it as your start-up money. Include the cost of the start-up kit as well as other business essentials, such as envelopes and business cards.

There are many other factors that can help you decide to spend more on your start-up costs. For example, if you have a large savings account and are looking to do this business as a retirement job, you might want to invest more up front so you can have a "quick" start. You might have a large life-insurance annuity that you can cash in to start the business.

The important thing is that the money you invest shouldn't be a drain on your finances. There is nothing wrong with the start-up costs "pinching" a little bit, but they should not put you and your family in any real financial jeopardy.

The Continual Investment

You also need to remember that business requires continual financial investment. You have to continue buying brochures and catalogs. Your computer will need replacing someday. Postage costs are constantly going up. You need printer paper. In most cases, you will need to buy new products as the company introduces them.

Be sure to figure those costs into your budget. A good way to do this is to set aside a certain percentage from every commission check you receive to help you build the business. You might start with 10 percent and see how that works out.

Then, as your business grows you can continue setting aside that percentage, but instead of using it all for "nuts and bolts" you will find that you have enough money to attend the company convention in Hawaii or to buy a new car for the business.

The Extent of Your Commitment

The vast majority of people start as part-time distributors and then decide to go full-time once they are comfortable with the product line and have built a fair-sized down-line. That works extremely well in network marketing because the vast majority of sales seem to take place outside of normal business hours. You can easily contact people in the evenings, on weekends, through the Internet, and by regular mail.

However, some people decide to jump right in full-time. You will know if this is right for you if you meet the following criteria:

- *Another family member makes enough money to pay your bills.* Be realistic. You certainly won't be making much money for at least a few months. Very few people make as much as they think they will for the first few years. As a result, you need someone who can pay at least the minimum bills for your family.
- *Another family member carries family health insurance.* Again, be realistic. Your network-marketing organization might offer health insurance to its top sellers, but it likely doesn't offer it to new distributors. Even if you're a healthy, robust college student, you could break a leg or need an emergency appendectomy. Remember that while health insurance is available to self-employed people, it can be very, very expensive.
- *You have sales experience.* In this case, you probably know exactly what you are getting into and can "jump-start" your business, ending up with good sales within the first few weeks.
- *You have a nest egg.* If you have enough money in savings to pay your bills for at least a year, you may be able to work your

network-marketing business full-time right from day one. This works especially well if you are retired or an empty-nest housewife and you want something to fill your days.

- *You have few other options.* Perhaps you have health issues that make it difficult to work outside the home and your community doesn't have many other work-at-home opportunities. In such a case, full-time network marketing could be the best thing for you.

Keeping a Professional Attitude

Whether it's part-time or full-time, network marketing is a job. You may dream of becoming a millionaire and never working again, but that isn't going to happen right away, even under the most lucrative plans in the best markets. Consequently, you have to work at seeing this as a job.

That can be a difficult step for some people, especially those who work at it only part-time. Some don't want to admit that they direct-sell for a living because they are afraid of the response they will get from other people. They want to think of this as a hobby that's just a fun way to meet people and get a little extra cash.

FACTS

If you act as though you have a job, people will start to view you in that light and you will start to feel as though you are a professional salesperson. Even if you are only involved in network marketing part-time, remind yourself that you are working.

Stay Disciplined

It's important to set regular work hours for yourself and stick to them, whether you feel like it or not. For example, if you are a housewife with young children, you might say that you will work on the business from 9 to 10 P.M. every night, Monday through Thursday. That's only four hours, but during that time you must be completely devoted to your job.

Make realistic goals for every week. For instance, make one new business contact or attend one of your up-line member's meetings every month. Or you might commit to making one presentation to a potential new distributor every week.

The goal here isn't to make sure those contacts turn into a sale. It's to keep you focused on work. If you're having a bad day and your one contact is to call a good customer and ask if she wants to buy anything this month, it's still a contact. Or maybe you send out a form letter to a neighbor telling him about the advantages of becoming a distributor. It's still a contact, even though it has little chance of success.

Communicating Your Decision

People will be curious about what you're up to. Your family and friends in particular will want to know why you got involved in network marketing and what you hope to get out of it. A few people might be concerned that you will try to pressure them into buying your products or joining your down-line. Others will think you're absolutely crazy.

Don't act overly enthusiastic about your new business venture, because people may think you have been brainwashed. Instead, you want to convey that you have thought this through and it's a sound business opportunity.

Never fear. You can't please everyone, so the best thing to do is to be honest. You're excited. You really want to do this. It's a life change. Whatever your reasons are, share them with your friends and family. You might find that people are more receptive than you think.

If you have trouble coming up with the best way of communicating your decision, here are some suggestions:

- Send a form letter to everyone on your holiday-card list.
- Send an e-mail to everyone on your e-mail list.
- Call your close family and friends to tell them the exciting news.
- Send a catalog with a short personal note to everyone you know.

- Put company signs on your car and in your yard.
- Include a short message about the products you are selling in your voice mail greeting.

You might also find that people are genuinely interested in the products you are selling. Remember that in today's fast-paced world, it's difficult for people to find the right products to meet all their needs. For example, if they're looking for safe, unusual children's toys and that's what your company offers, they may see your job change as a benefit for them.

If You Will Work Part-Time

If you're starting part-time, you can tell people that you really like the products, you've used them for several years, and you don't think there are enough people selling them.

You can even downplay the potential: "I don't expect to make big money, I just think it will be fun to meet people and I might as well get a little money back since I'm buying the products anyway."

Depending on your audience, you can talk about the "grassroots" approach to sales and how you like the idea that you are selling directly to your end-user with no big retail chain taking a cut of the profits.

You might also talk about wanting to try your hand at sales as a career and that you are using network marketing as your starting point. After all, even some of the world's top-paid salespeople got their start in network-marketing opportunities while in high school or college.

Another explanation might be a very simple: "I need the money and this is the only way I can find to make it work with our family situation." That works especially well if you're a housewife taking care of several young children.

If You Will Work Full-Time

If you're jumping right in to full-time work, the story might be a little more difficult to "sell" to your loved ones. They will be concerned about all the stories they hear about fraudulent pyramid schemes, so it's your job to reassure them that you have done your homework.

One method is to play up the "back door": "Look, I can always go back to work for a big corporation, but I really want to give this a try. I'm burned out at my job. I've checked out the company and they have a good, sound product." If you have followed the advice for checking out the company, you will most likely be able to convince anyone that you're making a fine decision.

ESSENTIALS

Not everyone will understand your decision, but don't let that bother you. Simply explain the facts and go on with your relationship with those people, just as though you took a new job working for someone else. Don't be overly enthusiastic about the opportunity with them, but don't shy away from discussing it either.

Another method for communicating a full-time commitment to network marketing is to tell people that it's always been your dream to work for yourself. And, again, if it doesn't work out, you have at least gained some valuable sales experience that you can take to another self-employment opportunity.

Telling the Difficult People

There may be a number of people in your life who will naturally find out what you are doing but whom you really don't want to tell because you know their reaction will be discouraging. In these situations, it's best to go with a piece of wisdom handed down through the ages: The less said the better. Something like, "I've decided to start a new business opportunity, selling XYZ" should be enough information.

QUESTIONS?

What do I do if people I really care about start telling me I'm making the biggest mistake of my life?
Revisit your research on the company and reassure yourself that this is a good opportunity—then work to prove them wrong.

It's Not the Right Time to Sell

When you share your news, don't try to talk anyone into buying anything just yet. In fact, you might want to change the subject fairly soon in the conversation, just to allay their fears that you will become a high-pressure salesperson. Say something like, "I've just always wanted to try something like this and I'm excited about this product so I'm going to give it a try. Now, what's new with you?"

Staying Connected

As you move into your new job, it's important to stay connected to your family, friends, and former coworkers. You don't want to become a company person who associates only with people from the company and goes to visit people only if it has to do with company business.

One reason for this is that you never know when a person will consider joining your down-line. You may suddenly find that a friend loses her job and comes to you asking for information about how to join your company.

Even more important, however, is that you are doing this in part to gain control over your life. You don't want to give up what you have already achieved in your life. In fact, you should be as disciplined about getting away from work as you are about having a "job" attitude. Schedule at least one lunch with an old friend every month. Set aside an evening a week to go on a date with your spouse. Take Sunday afternoons and spend them with the kids.

During these times, be sure to revel in the world. Enjoy yourself. Don't talk business, even if the good friend you're having lunch with looks like a perfect candidate for your down-line. There's always tomorrow to contact him. In the meantime, remind yourself that you are creating the life you want.

CHAPTER 11

Time Management

The secret to success in any business endeavor is using your time wisely. You don't have to be a sales wizard or a business genius to succeed in network marketing as long as you keep working at it productively. Organize yourself, lose those time-wasting habits, and replace them with new, more productive ones.

Organize Your Workspace

If you've never been in business for yourself, you're in for a big surprise. Remember that you now hold every position in the company, from receptionist and delivery person to chief executive officer. As a result, you need an office space that reflects these many different titles.

The good news is that you have many options. So many people are pursuing work-at-home activities that the makers of business equipment are responding with everything from desks to filing systems that make organization easy even in the smallest office space.

For example, many people just starting out will keep their entire "office" in a few portable filing boxes. When it's time to work, they pull them out of the closet and it takes just seconds to set up a productive workspace.

However, even those who are lucky enough to have an entire room set aside as their office will need to learn good time-management skills to make their business a success. No matter how professional your surroundings look, if you don't use them well, you won't be productive.

The Family Attitude

The key to making a home office work is to have a dedicated workspace at specific times. If you use your kitchen table for a desk, that's fine as long as the family knows that it's off-limits to them during your work hours. Likewise, you can use a corner of the living room, your bedroom, or any other space as long as everyone knows that this is your office.

If you can close a door, that's wonderful. If not, some people buy portable screens that mark off their workspace. Others will put up a sign that reads "WORKING. DO NOT DISTURB!"

FACTS

Your family and friends will respect your work time as long as you act as though you're working. Don't let them disturb you and they will soon come to understand that this is as much of a job as if you commuted to an office every day.

If you don't have a family, that takes some pressure off, but it's still up to you to enforce the "at work" rule. That means you need to keep visits from friends down to a minimum and avoid long phone conversations. And—most importantly—don't get distracted by housework or other chores.

As long as you are dedicated to this job, it usually takes just a couple of weeks to "train" the important people in your life. Your parents will quickly learn that if they call during your work hours, you will sound preoccupied and will cut the conversation short. Your children will learn that you will get cranky if they interrupt you and you will refuse to deal with anything but the direst emergency until you're done with work.

And, secretly, most of those people will be happy to comply with your request for annoyance-free work time. After all, they want you to succeed and, by staying away from you during your dedicated work hours, they can actually feel as though they are helping you.

If you are planning to purchase a desk for your workspace, think small. Large desks are just a place to store clutter that can get lost and distract you. A smaller desk encourages you to get the work done because the papers keep getting in your way!

A Filing System

To help keep yourself organized, you should set up a filing system that will give you easy access to lots of information. If you have a filing cabinet, that's wonderful, although plastic file boxes are nice because you can take them with you—and they make great footrests if you're tired of sitting in one position! Consider keeping your files organized by topic. Here are some you will probably find useful:

- *The product background.* This file will contain all your product information and company updates. You can also include any scientific studies about the products as well as any general background on the growing need for the type of items you sell.
- *Marketing materials.* This file will contain all the current catalogs and brochures as well as copies of your or your sponsor's newsletters and

testimonials. Anything you use to convince people to buy your products or to become distributors should be included here.

- *Current customers.* You should have a file for each customer, even if he or she has purchased from you only once. Keep each customer's name, address, and phone number, and information about their buying preferences.
- *Prospective customers.* Keep a list of people you plan to contact as potential customers and any contact information you have for them.
- *Prospective distributors.* You will find it useful to keep a list of all those who have shown some interest in becoming a distributor for your company.
- *Business expenses.* Keep track of all your business expenses by filing away all receipts, mileage records, phone bills, insurance expenses, photocopying fees, and so on, which will be important for filing your taxes the following spring.
- *Legal documents.* Use this folder for storing the contract you signed with your company, tax forms, and other legal contracts or documents.

SSENTIALS   Set up a "business strategies" folder, a catchall file for magazine articles, company training materials, and anything else you find that might help you with your business. Another idea is to create a personal folder, which might contain inspirational notes and articles about how to balance work with the rest of your life.

Set Your Goals

Goals are the most important ingredient in time management because they tell you how much time to spend in any given area. Maybe your ultimate goal is to become a millionaire within ten years. That's nice, but how will you get there? You will take it one step at a time.

Set Daily Goals

Daily goals are those you should accomplish *today*. They are the little details of any business that must be taken care of on a daily basis in order to keep everything running. Ideally, you will get all your daily goals done before you go to bed, but don't overburden yourself. You want to make progress, but you don't have to burn yourself out with these goals.

When you make a list of your daily goals, also include some personal ones. Do you want to spend at least five hours a day playing with your children? Add that to the list. Do you want to call your hospitalized mother once a day? It may seem heartless at first, but once you get into the rhythm of it, you'll notice that it's just a reminder to keep your goals in mind.

Weekly Goals

Weekly goals should be oriented more toward business development, though some of them should still focus on getting things done in a timely way. Some weekly goals are really a breakdown of monthly goals, which are larger in scope. Some examples of these are setting up a prospecting system or learning a new computer program.

Don't make your goals too difficult to achieve. You can always find something to fill your time if you achieve your goals for the day, week, or month, but you will just get frustrated if you have too many goals that are impossible to accomplish.

Include personal goals in your weekly goals, too. Perhaps you want to have one formal dinner with your family every week. Or maybe you want to volunteer at your child's school. Singles might want to sign up for a class or do something else that gets them involved in nonwork activities and allows them to meet new people.

Long-Term Goals

Every network marketer should have annual and lifetime goals. Perhaps you want to reach a certain sales level by the end of the year. Or maybe you want to transition from part-time to full-time as a network marketer by the end of the year. And what about that goal of becoming a millionaire within the next ten years?

Often, these goals will mesh with your personal goals. You want to have the money set aside to send junior to college within five years. You want to have a new house within three years. You want to be financially independent within ten years.

On a daily basis, these goals are only good for motivation. You can't actually do anything about becoming a millionaire in ten years today, this week, or even this month. However, if you post these goals on your desk so you can see them at all times, they will remind you to set your more immediate goals appropriately so that one day you can meet these long-term objectives.

FACTS

Any goal is achievable if you break it into smaller, more easily accomplished parts. If a goal seems overwhelming, just go back to the basic steps: Pick up the phone, or turn on the computer, or head for the door. Soon you will find yourself ready for the next easy step, and before you know it, you will have met the goal.

Set Your Vision

There's a lot of talk these days about a company's or an individual's vision. It sounds kind of hokey, but it's extremely important, especially when you are in business for yourself. Your vision is what keeps you motivated when days get tough. It's what gets you through the boring work.

A vision is literally something you can visualize. You can sit back in your desk chair when you're having a tough day, close your eyes, and see yourself living your vision. Your vision is your guiding force and you should work hard to develop a vision that truly represents what you want to achieve with your life.

Many people define their vision in terms of possessions. They want a certain car, a certain house, and a certain amount of money in their kids' college bank accounts. That's not a bad way to do it if you're so inclined. You could even get pictures of those items and post them around your workspace so that every time you wonder why you're doing this, you can look up and see.

Other people get into network marketing because it lets them have more freedom and more time with their family, and helps them feel like they are doing something good for the world. For example, one company that sells herbal products hires indigenous people to harvest herbs and wild fruit from the rain forest, protecting the local habitat and providing the local population with health and social services.

Whatever your vision is, write it down in one sentence and display it where you can look up and read it while you work. Your brain will literally "see" this future for you and motivate you to work toward it.

A Goal or a Vision?

The difference between your goals and your vision is that the goals are concrete work tasks or achievements. Goals are the specific things you want to achieve on your way to reaching your vision. You want to have $1 million in the bank in ten years: That's a goal. Your vision would be how you want to live with that money.

QUESTIONS?

I don't really have a vision. I just want to get rich. Is that a problem?
Not necessarily, but chances are you do have some type of vision. Ask yourself what you want to do after you are rich, and it will become clear.

That's why goals drive your prioritizing every second you work. They are the direct outcome of your work. As a result, every time you wonder if you should do one thing or another today, you turn to your goals and the answer is right there.

Goals change constantly, while your vision should stay the same. Think of it this way: You know what you want your life to look like in ten years, but other people, world events, health issues, and many other factors get in the way as roadblocks for getting there. You have to alter your path but you still have the same destination in mind.

The Value of Lists

Lists are a wonderful way to manage your time. They will help you keep track of what you need to get done and see how you are progressing with all your chores. Try developing several lists on every Monday morning. They might include some of the following:

- Emergency stuff
- The day's work
- The week's work
- The month's work
- Extra work (in case all other obligations are met)

Keep your daily list posted right in front of you at all times. As the day progresses, you get to cross out the items that you have completed, which will give you a real sense of accomplishment and encourage you to work further.

How to Prioritize

Once you have your to-do lists, it's important to be able to prioritize—figure out which tasks need to be accomplished first. Don't fall into the trap of trying to complete all the little, menial tasks before going on to do the important stuff. The menial tasks will never end—there is always another envelope to stuff, another form to fill out, and another phone call to make—and you'll never get to doing any of the more important projects on your list. Another mistake is to do everything on your to-do list in the order that it appears.

The easiest way to prioritize activities is by looking at what each activity will accomplish, whether it's landing a new distributor, prospecting for new customers, selling to regular customers, or keeping up with paperwork.

Quit While You Still Have Energy

Some people run and run and run until they are completely burned out. That's okay when you're in college and have exams or papers due, but it's not the way to run a business. There is always more work to do when you are self-employed, but you have to learn to quit before you're too tired or you will be too tired to enjoy your life.

Just as you have to discipline yourself to work at least an hour a day, you may also have to discipline yourself not to work. Just tell yourself that no matter how important something is on your to-do list, you will not work after midnight, for example.

At this point, go back to your personal goals for direction. You want flexibility as well as financial independence. If you're working so hard that you don't have time for your family, you're not meeting your goals.

It's also important to realize that a good night's sleep can make a world of difference in meeting your goals. For example, if you're struggling to complete your paperwork at 2 A.M., you might find that it's easier to complete it at 8 A.M., after a good night's sleep.

Get It Right the First Time

Don't set out on a project until you have a good idea of how you will proceed. Most successful people say they have to "get it in their head first." That means they want to think it through so that they know exactly what they are going to do.

For example, if you're working on building your prospect list, don't just start adding names to the list; you will probably get stuck quite early in the process. Think about where you can get the best names—the PTA members, your church directory, the Rotary Club, your Toastmasters group, and so on. Then you can quickly get the lists.

"Doing it right" might mean that you can't meet your goal quite as quickly as you would like because you have to spend time researching how you will meet it. For example, you might not get that marketing piece out this week because you first have to learn how to use the software to create it. If that worries you, keep this in mind: The time you spend making sure you are doing something right will save you the time and trouble of redoing it in the end.

As you think about working your business, always look for the most efficient way to do something. You work for yourself now. You can't waste even a second, because that second could be the one that makes you a millionaire.

CHAPTER 12

Help Along the Way

Network marketing is a business like any other. To keep it running smoothly, you will need to have the right tools and experts you can turn to if you have problems. Set boundaries and establish relationships at the beginning so there are no surprises as your business grows.

Tools to Make Your Job Easier

It's difficult to accomplish any task without having the right tools, so what tools do you need to be successful in network marketing? You have already learned about the advantages of having an organized workspace in Chapter 11. But you also need to consider your other home-office needs. A separate phone line, a computer with a printer and access to the Internet, and other office equipment will surely make your job a lot easier.

The Phone

In this business, your phone is your most valuable ally, but chances are, your current phone system is inadequate for running a business. It's best to have a separate phone line for your business. It makes keeping track of phone expenses easier and you can have a professional greeting on the answering machine. Most importantly, your six-year-old won't have to take messages from your customers and your thirteen-year-old won't tie up the phone for hours.

Avoid the temptation to get lots of bells and whistles on your phone system. You need to be able to record everyone's calls and ensure they don't get a busy signal—and that's it. Other options can be more annoying than helpful.

It's also a good idea to have a voice mail option through your phone company rather than an actual answering machine. That way, if you are talking on the phone, additional callers will be forwarded to voice mail and can leave you messages.

If you have call waiting, disconnect it immediately. There is nothing more irritating to a customer than to hear the incessant beeping of call waiting or, worse yet, to have you put him or her on hold as you answer another person's call.

Caller ID is another good option because it lets you quickly see if a call is worth taking—whether the person calling is a good customer, your sponsor, a prospect, or a telemarketer. If you're in the middle of something that takes concentration, such as filing orders for the month, you can easily determine if it is a call you must take immediately or if you can get back to the person in a few minutes.

Computer and Printer

If you can afford it, a computer is your best bet for both storing information and for writing letters and other materials. If you think you can't afford a computer, try renting one through a business supply store or buying a used machine. Today's new computers are extremely powerful and frequently have features you don't really need to run your business.

FACTS

You can probably find a computer that will meet your needs for about $500. Look for models that are about two years old. They offer enough memory and power to run all but the most sophisticated business software.

You can also consider purchasing a printer, although it's not too difficult to get by without one. To print, all you need to do is save your work on a CD or a floppy disk and take it to a local print shop. On the other hand, printers are very inexpensive, in some cases less than $100; if you have the space and money, having a printer is a convenience. You can print information off the Web and dash off quick letters without having to take a trip every time you need something printed.

Business Stationery

If you do buy a printer, you will also need to stock up on stationery. Your network-marketing company will probably give you some advice on getting letterhead and envelopes. Some companies even supply their salespeople with these products at a reduced price.

Most business stationery can be made right on your computer. Even envelopes and business cards can be printed with today's high-quality, low-cost inkjet printers.

Business Cards

Business cards are another matter. Your company may provide them at a small cost—some companies will even insist that you have business cards that follow their format. If that isn't the case, you can print them on your computer. However, for less than $20, most business supply stores and small print shops will make 500 business cards specifically for you. These will look a lot more professional than home-printed versions and you can include a company logo or any information you would like.

Remember that even in today's electronic age, people like to have a physical reminder of you. Although you may think you can get by without business cards, they are essential.

Internet Access

Many companies offer online ordering, strategies for helping you prospect online, and even allow you to host a Web site to help you make your sales and attract distributors. If you want to take advantage of these services, you will need to sign up with an Internet provider.

It is possible to get free Internet access, but these services are often unreliable and are jam-packed with advertising that may slow you down (if you have an older computer, all those pop-up windows may actually cause your machine to crash periodically, wasting your time and patience). You are better off paying about $30 a month for one of the standard services such as AOL or Earthlink, which are faster and more reliable.

If you live in a small town, you may find that your long-distance bills rise dramatically when you start using the Internet. Try finding a long-distance phone company that offers reduced rates at certain times of the day and restrict your usage of the Internet to those times.

However, these services are provided through your phone line, so you won't be able to log on and use your phone at the same time (yet another good reason for getting that voice mail service). If you don't want to tie up your phone line, you'll have to get a DSL (direct service link), which will keep you online at all times; however, DSL services are still quite costly and aren't available outside of large communities.

Get Help from the Experts

We can't do everything ourselves—that's why we have experts in the world. Yes, you could research all the health-insurance options available to you, or you could hire a consultant to do it for you. Chances are, your time is more valuable prospecting for new business, because that's what you're good at. Sometimes it makes sense to pay people to do the work they're good at.

Here is a list of experts you might need to turn to for help at some point in your network-marketing career:

- Lawyers
- Accountants
- Insurance consultants
- Clerical workers
- Sales trainers

These people can save you a lot of money because they know how to get something done quickly. They have the expertise and access to the tools that help them to do the job right. You simply can't replace the information available to a lawyer, accountant, or insurance consultant.

Likewise, you could read dozens of sales-training books every month, or you could ask around, find a good sales trainer, and spend two days taking a course. A sales trainer has already sifted through all the information out there and found the gems. You can take advantage of his or her experience and spend your time doing what you are best at—selling.

Legal Assistance

It's likely that one day you will need to turn to an attorney for legal assistance, whether it's to ask for advice on a particular legal subject, to help you draw a contract or a legal agreement, or—though this isn't very likely—because you are involved in a lawsuit. Don't wait until a problem comes up and you need legal assistance right away. You can prepare today by finding a good attorney you know you can turn to.

Although choosing an attorney is an important issue for your business, it does not have to be time-consuming or costly. The easiest approach to take is to ask your sponsor and others in your sponsor's down-line for a recommendation.

ESSENTIALS

> Most lawsuits don't go to court because they simply aren't good cases. You want a lawyer who won't spend your money until she knows that the person suing is serious and that his or her lawyer thinks it's a good lawsuit.

Here are a few questions you might ask when you talk to a prospective lawyer:

- *Do you understand and respect network marketing as a business?* Your attorney should know what network marketing entails and should recognize it as a legitimate business endeavor. However, don't expect your lawyer to be familiar with the details of your company.
- *Do you have many other self-employed clients in direct sales?* If this attorney doesn't have other salespeople as clients, you might want to look for someone else. The attorney may be very good at business law but not understand the special liability issues and other concerns that a salesperson has.
- *Do you handle personal and business concerns?* It's convenient to have an attorney who can help you with both your business and your personal matters.
- *What is your philosophy when working on a case?* Some attorneys like to be proactive if someone sues you. They will file documents,

write letters, and in general burn up hours and dollars. That is probably not the type of attorney you want. Instead, you want an attorney who believes in collecting everything sent to him or her and responding only when absolutely necessary.

Service Charges

Be sure to find out how your attorney charges for services. Some attorneys ask for a yearly or monthly retainer, for which they will perform routine services that are outlined in a contract. Others will do only the work you ask them to perform and charge you a flat fee. Still others will charge an hourly fee for consultations (this includes phone conversations) as well as work such as filing legal documents.

You can look over the options and decide what best meets your needs. However, it's likely that in the first stages of your business, you will want to pay for some consultation time. This lets the attorney advise you on matters such as the language in your contract with your parent company and in your insurance contracts. The attorney can also help you if you plan to hire staff at some point or if you want to incorporate your business.

Accounting Services

You will also need the services of a professional accountant. While many attorneys have a solid background in tax law, the accountant will know the details of filing your taxes correctly. He or she is more likely to be up to date on deductions and other tax information. Like the lawyer, the accountant can tell you what will save you money in the long run, so think of paying for the accountant's advice as a good investment.

You don't need to spend a great deal of money on an accountant. Many small-business owners hire an accountant to help them set up their bookkeeping systems and then visit them once a year to re-examine the system and to file taxes.

Again, ask other people in your business who they use for their accounting and then interview a couple of these people to see who you like best. When you talk to prospective accountants, ask the following questions:

- *Do you work with many small-business owners?* If the answer is no, look for someone else. The self-employed have many tax benefits that large corporations don't have, and vice versa.
- *Do you understand network marketing?* It's especially important that your accountant understands how network marketing works, because he or she will be reporting your income and expenses on your taxes.
- *How do you charge for your services?* Accountants charge much like attorneys. You likely will want a few hours of consultation when you first set up your business, but probably can go with a flat fee for services after that.

FACTS

Bookkeeping and accounting are not the same tasks. Bookkeeping involves keeping track of all your financial transactions. The accountant can oversee bookkeeping, file taxes, and offer financial advice to his or her clients.

Bookkeeping Issues

Your job entails more than meeting people and making sales. You also need to keep track of all those little details. And let's not kid ourselves—bookkeeping can be a real pain.

It's very important that you do your paperwork correctly. Your primary concern should be your taxes—you have to ensure that you are recording all of your income and all of your expenses accurately so that you have all the information ready when the time comes to file your tax forms. Furthermore, you have to keep those records so that if you are audited, you can prove that everything you claimed was legitimate. More than one small-business owner has paid hundreds of thousands of dollars in extra taxes because he or she didn't keep correct books.

You also want to have a good bookkeeping system for personal reasons. You want to make sure you are charging people correctly for their orders and that you are being paid correctly for your work and the work of your down-line. You want to be able to look up your transactions if someone has a question so that you can resolve any disputes.

Where to Turn for Help

There are several computer software programs for small businesses that do an excellent job with bookkeeping. Most community colleges also offer basic bookkeeping courses for small-business owners.

Another option is to hire someone to do this work for you. It could be a professional bookkeeper or a family member who enjoys working with numbers. Remember that if you hire a family member, he or she can file taxes as though self-employed, assuming the criteria are met.

Hiring Family and Friends

Whatever help you might need in the course of your career as a network marketer—from finding legal help to getting a paid filing service—it'll always be easier to hire family and friends. After all, you know them and they know you. Why wouldn't you extend your relationship by offering work in return for payment?

As you set up your business, remember that you want to use other people wherever you can so that you can concentrate on bringing in more business. Let others do what they like and you will be able to do what you like more often.

Before you go ahead and extend such an offer, take a moment to think about it. Self-employed people can get into a great deal of trouble when they hire family and friends to work for them. There are, of course, advantages—especially when hiring family members. If you hire your daughter to do your bookkeeping, for example, she can then claim that she is self-employed and enjoy all the tax benefits that brings. She could also begin doing bookkeeping work for people in your down-line and bring in even more college money.

However, an employee is an employee. Every working relationship has a legal component to it. Work with a human resources consultant or your lawyer to draw up contracts for friends and families who are taking over duties such as clerical work. These contracts can be simple, but they should specify what work needs to be done to get paid and should waive you of any responsibility for mistakes the person makes.

Even if you decide not to have contracts, be sure you make it clear that you are hiring your friend or family member to do a job. You are paying a fair wage, and you expect the work to get done according to your needs and in a timely fashion.

CHAPTER 13

Keeping Your Spirits High

It all seemed so easy when you saw your sponsor doing it. Now that you're on your own, though, it seems a little tougher. Don't worry! There are time-proven strategies for making it through those first weeks of a new job. You know you can do it, and you have a group of people who can help you keep up your morale.

Recognizing Your Strengths

Now that you've made the decision to start on this path and the excitement is starting to wear down, it's time to make an honest assessment of what you are good and not so good at. Do some soul-searching on each of these topics:

- Meeting new people
- Bookkeeping and paperwork
- Following up on details
- Acting enthusiastic (even when tired and depressed)
- Reading nonverbal cues
- Understanding what different personality types want
- Quickly understanding product features and benefits
- Creatively looking for new prospects
- Motivating people
- Speaking in front of a group
- Being genuine (as opposed to acting like a slick salesperson)
- Learning new computer software
- Balancing work and fun

No one, absolutely no one, is good at all these things, yet they are all important to the job. Rate each item on a scale from 1 to 3:

1 = you're very good at this task
2 = you can get by
3 = you're not very good at it

Now look at all those things you are good at. They are the strengths from which you can build. For example, if you are good at motivating people, you might want to consider quickly building a large down-line. If you like to meet new people, making cold calls should feel natural to you.

In some cases, if you find that you are good at something, you can just cross it off the list of skills necessary for the job. Paperwork is a good example of this. If you are good at paperwork, you will have no trouble getting your orders right and in on time, so it's something you don't have to worry about.

SSENTIALS Save your assessment of yourself and revisit it one year later. You may be surprised how many more items have moved up to 1s or 2s on the list. Then put your new assessment in your personal file!

Working on Your Weaknesses

Every person has weaknesses. Look at Bill Gates, for example. He's shy, doesn't read nonverbal cues very well, and doesn't like to meet new people. You'd never guess, though, because today he does all those activities extremely well. The reason is that he looked at his goals and saw that he couldn't reach them without becoming at least proficient in these areas.

You can do the same. Let's say you love the prospect of selling but you hate paperwork. Well, the first step is to recognize this in yourself. Then, try to find a way to work through it. Perhaps you will hire someone else to do the paperwork. Perhaps you will just set aside a couple of hours every week and force yourself to get it done. Perhaps you will take a course that shows you how to do your paperwork more efficiently.

ALERT Do not focus too heavily on your weaknesses during the first weeks of work. Concentrate on your strengths and work to improve your weaknesses gradually as you become more comfortable with your new job.

Maybe you're comfortable with selling but aren't sure how to motivate people in your down-line. After all, selling comes naturally to you so you've never thought about it. Again, try to find a solution that will work for you. For instance, see if you can find another distributor who does a good job at motivating his or her down-line and get some good ideas.

The important thing is that you are aware of your weaknesses and are willing to work with them. Otherwise they will start to take over your work and you will fail.

First-Month Jitters

Everybody is nervous when they first take on a new job. Working for yourself can be even worse, because no one is telling you what to do. No one is setting deadlines for you. No one is telling you if you're doing a good job or if you need improvement. The world suddenly seems very large and remote.

Inevitably, you'll find that things don't go the way you thought they would. Sales aren't as easy to make. People aren't as receptive to the product as you thought they would be. You just lost all your prospects because the computer crashed. Your kids, who promised to give you work space, have been driving you crazy.

The most important thing to do is relax. If you researched this opportunity well and you're enthusiastic about it, you'll do just fine. It does no good to second-guess your decision at this point; on the contrary, it could do a lot of harm. If you're too busy wondering if you made a mistake, you won't have time to be productive and get things done.

Breaking Through the Brick Wall

Suddenly you're frightened to pick up the phone to make a sales call. The idea of making a presentation terrifies you. You sit at your desk, knowing you should be working on developing a prospect list, but all you can do is play solitaire on the computer.

You start to panic. You don't know why you can't seem to get any work done. You want to work, but it just isn't happening.

It's called a *brick wall*, and it happens to everyone in sales. Just as actors get stage fright, writers get writer's block, and artists go into "funks," salespeople hit brick walls. Sometimes it means you arrived at a turning point in your career and you don't know what to do next.

If you're in the first weeks of your business, you're probably hitting the wall because you're suddenly on your own. Your sponsor has helped you get started and you've made a lot of important decisions about how you will run the business, but now you have to get down to the daily grind of actually doing the work.

The key to breaking through the brick wall is to just get to work. Look at your desk, take a big breath, take out a pad of paper, and start making your day's to-do list. That will get you in the right frame of mind.

FACTS

Any work is progress. Don't be concerned if you can only muster the enthusiasm to do the simplest activities. As long as you are working at the business, you will make progress toward your goals.

Preparing to Break Through

Still don't feel like working? Take the easiest thing on the to-do list and break it into the most ridiculously simple steps you can think of. You might start with something as simple as adding five names to your new prospect list. This is how you might break down this task:

1. Get out the new prospect file and open it.
2. Think of three people you recently met.
3. Put their names on Prospect Information Forms (which are found inside the file).
4. Determine how to find their phone numbers or addresses.
5. Add the information about how you will find their phone numbers or addresses to the forms.
6. Cross off that activity from your to-do list.

Granted, it wasn't much, but you can say you did something, right? You might not have started breaking down the brick wall with this project, but you did get the courage to grab the metaphorical hammer and chisel and start walking toward the wall.

The First Chip at the Wall

Next, pick something just slightly more difficult from the to-do list. For example, if you want to call three people about buying from you, the steps might be:

1. Open the new prospect file.
2. Find three names of people you know really well but who probably won't be home. (After all, you're a bit panicky. You certainly don't really want to talk to anyone at this point.)
3. Rehearse a short message for their machines: "Hi, John, it's Suzanne Smith. I'm selling XYZ now and was wondering if I could talk to you about it."
4. Make the calls, leave the messages, and cross that project off your to-do list.

It doesn't seem as though you did much, does it? You knew the people wouldn't be home and it's not as though you left a convincing message. Still, you got your working blood pumping. You made a tiny chip in that great big brick wall. Chances are, you will be able to tackle the next, slightly harder project on your to-do list.

Just remember to stay committed and continue working. You might be nervous or even downright terrified when you encounter a new situation, but countless people have worked through these fears before, and you know you can, too.

When Things Go Wrong

You will make mistakes. The company will make mistakes. You will wonder why you ever decided to do this. You'll wonder if you should quit and move to another state.

It happens. You charge someone too much for a product and they get unreasonably angry. The company sends a product that is out of date or doesn't work. The customer, your former best friend, blames you for talking him into buying from a shoddy company. You forget to attend an important meeting and your sponsor calls you up to say some not-too-friendly things.

Ah, life as a small-business owner is not always fun because the buck truly does stop with you. While you can blame others—such as the distribution department at the network-marketing company—your customers will blame you and only you.

The key is not to blame yourself. You can't be perfect. You certainly are entitled to a few mathematical errors. You can't possibly go to the factory where your products are manufactured to make sure they are sending you what you ordered. And, yes, you probably should have looked at your calendar so you would make that important meeting, but you were so stressed out that you simply forgot.

At times like these, you need to get into recovery mode. Do whatever you can to fix the situation. Apologize. Promise to do better. Apologize again. Promise to make amends. Write a letter of apology. Give the customer the product for free. Apologize. You get the point.

Then forget that it happened. You can't change the past; you can only move forward. If someone brings up what happened, apologize again, but then tell them that you've done everything you can to make the situation right. If they are still angry at you, forget about it for a while.

Remember that things go wrong. You can't control the whole world and you are not perfect. Work to resolve the situation and then go on with your life. Learn from your mistakes, but don't dwell on them.

Your sponsor will certainly cool down. A rational customer will eventually forgive you. An irrational customer won't, but it's probably not worth your time and effort to have such people as customers anyway.

The Power of Affirmations

Many self-help groups use daily affirmations to help their members overcome problems. Many salespeople rely on affirmations in their work—as silly as it might sound, telling yourself something often enough forces you to really believe it.

More than likely your company offers its salespeople affirmations and supportive messages on stickers or pieces of cardboard that you can post around your office. If the company doesn't, try some of these generic ones:

- "I love working for myself."
- "I can do it, I can do it, I can do it!"
- "I am strong, smart, creative, and driven to succeed."

You can also come up with your own affirmations. To keep these messages visible, you can post them around your workspace or your home. Here are some ideas:

- Post them around your work area so you can see one every time you look away from the computer.
- Put one on the dashboard of your car.
- Keep a list in your wallet and read them right before a sales call.
- Keep one pasted to your phone.
- Use them as bookmarks.
- Post one on your bathroom mirror.
- Put one on your nightstand so you read it just before you turn off the lights to go to bed, and again first thing in the morning.

The Kudos File

Another type of affirmation is a file that contains your every working success. When you're feeling especially low, pull out this file and remind yourself how good you really are. Here are a few ideas for what you might include:

- Congratulatory notes from your sponsor and others in your up-line
- Notes of praise from customers
- Copies of your biggest sales orders

- A list of all the people you have ever sold to
- The dates you reached big achievements, such as sales goals, number of people in your down-line, number of customers, and so on

In the beginning, you may not have much related to network marketing to keep in your kudos file. That's okay. You can add kudos items from past jobs as well as notes and mementos of your achievements in high school or college. Whatever makes you feel good about yourself and your work ethic should go into this file.

Review your kudos file every day before you start work. Pull out one memo or memento that makes you especially proud. Remind yourself that you were good then and you will be good again.

The Personal File

Yet another type of affirmation you need to keep nearby is your personal file. This will include everything about your life that you love so that you can constantly be reminded of what is important to you.

Notes and drawings from your children, photographs, and other keepsakes could serve as inspirations and a reminder of your priorities on those slump days. If you are religious, you might want to include specific religious passages in this file or even a simple note that reminds you: "God wants me to succeed."

Do not under any circumstances look at your long-term goals when your work isn't going as well as expected. This will make you only more depressed and anxious. Focus instead on the good things in life—what you already have and what you are already blessed with.

Working with Your Sponsor

Your sponsor should be a major source of help during these first few weeks. Remember that your sponsor has been through it all already and likely has helped other new distributors through these first weeks as well.

As a result, don't hesitate to call him or her whenever you are nervous or "hit the wall." Tell your sponsor flat out that you need to be reminded that you can do this. If you feel the need, ask her to meet you at a local café for a cup of coffee.

You can look to your sponsor for good advice on how to break through the brick wall and depend on her to guide you through difficult situations. For example, if you are having a panic attack about hosting your first sales party, ask your sponsor to come along for moral support.

Since your sponsor has been in this business longer than you, maybe he has a favorite book or video that is motivating to new salespeople. If not, go shopping at a local bookstore together to find one.

You will probably feel remarkably better after having contact with your sponsor again. It's possible that all you really need is a word of encouragement, a phrase like "I know you can do it," and you will feel the adrenaline rushing through your bloodstream again.

SSENTIALS

Your sponsor is your mentor and should be there for you at all times. Don't hesitate to contact your sponsor as much as you need to during the first weeks. There are no dumb questions and no silly needs—if you took the time to find a good sponsor, you should feel no qualms about going to her with questions or requests.

Fast or Slow—It's Up to You

Many sponsors like to see their new distributors get a fast start. They believe that success breeds more success. It's a good strategy for many people because they end up being so busy right from the beginning that they don't have time to have second thoughts.

In these cases, the sponsor will "seed" your customer list by giving you a couple of his good customers as well as a couple of his hot prospects. These "guaranteed" sales make you so enthusiastic and confident that you just keep on making more and more sales.

Other people prefer a slow start, though. If that's your personality, you will know because you will find that you want to learn about the product thoroughly and become comfortable selling it to just one or two close friends or family members before you branch out.

Surprisingly, many of the world's top salespeople for big-name companies are actually slow starters. They are very thorough and want to make sure they get it right. Once they do get it right, there is no stopping them, because they never have to back up to learn more sales skills or more about the product.

If you are a slow starter, don't be concerned. Your sponsor may try to push you to make sales, but that's okay because you will learn from that, too. Simply take these first weeks at your own pace and you'll do fine.

The Basic Sales Script

Confidence comes from being prepared. To get you started with the most basic strategy of selling, let's review a basic sales script. You can use this script to make sales calls or sales presentations.

Perhaps your network-marketing company has offered you sales training and helped you come up with a sales script. If not, you will want to create one for yourself. It will come in very handy when it's time for you to open your mouth and speak.

When you are preparing your basic sales script, you want to come up with and then memorize a few key concepts that you plan to present. Try to avoid actually creating a polished speech that you can rattle off at a moment's notice. Salespeople call this a "canned" presentation, and it will inevitably fail because people can tell that you are reciting something.

For example, if your product is all-natural, you want to talk about how it is made and why this quality is important. You know exactly what you want to say and possibly how you want to say it, but you will change it slightly each time you make your presentation.

The Introduction

Your first few sentences during any sales call are extremely important. They will establish that you know what you are doing and will set the tone for the rest of the presentation. With that in mind, these should be fairly well rehearsed and include specific information, no matter who you are selling to.

Your first comments should cover who you are, how you got involved with selling for your company, and why you personally like the products. This should be fairly short and to the point, but also tailored to the situation. For example, if the customer is your family member, you can skip a self-description but might go into greater detail about how you came to sell the product and what you like about it.

Next you will need to provide some information about the company—how the company was founded, what its mission is, and how long it has been in business. You don't need to go into great detail because you are just trying to establish that this business is legitimate. If it is a brand-new opportunity, you might want to go into a little more detail than if the company is a household name.

You should also talk about the benefits that apply to all the products. Some examples are:

- Manufactured in the United States
- All-natural
- Scientifically proven to be better than competitors
- Used for more than 100 years

Finally, mention something about the benefits of becoming a distributor, although this doesn't have to come at the beginning of the presentation. Likely your sponsor has told you a good "soft sell" tactic that works well, such as mentioning that if they like the product they can get it for 25 percent off by becoming a distributor.

Friends or Strangers?

If the person is a friend, your job is fairly easy because you likely know enough about the person to decide what you want to cover without thinking about it too much. The key with a friend, though, is to not be so enthusiastic that the person begins to think you are trying to take advantage of the friendship. In fact, you may try being a little softer with your sales pitch to good friends, telling them that you're excited about these products and you want to show them what it's all about but that you "certainly wouldn't expect them to buy anything."

FACTS

Strangers can actually be easier to present to because you don't care as much what they think about you. Ask your sponsor to set you up with at least one cold call during your first couple weeks so you can see the difference between selling to friends and strangers.

If it's a group of strangers, you will want to figure out what they all have in common—are they all young women, do they live in the same neighborhood, are they all married, or do they have similar income and education levels?

If you know nothing about the group, ask the person hosting the event to fill you in a little bit. For example, you don't want to be talking to a wealthy group of women about how your product can save them as much as $10 a year on their laundry costs!

Make a list of the things you think the group will be interested in. You don't have to hit this perfectly because you will be able to judge their interest more as you're actually talking to them.

If you sell a large line of products, pull out the dozen or so that you have decided to feature to this group based on what you know about them. (Be sure they represent the basic product categories.)

If you are selling to an individual, you will do the exact same thing, but will try to tailor the presentation even more. List everything you know about the person, then decide what items or benefits you will present.

Have several choices on your list so that if the person doesn't seem interested in one subject or product you can quickly move to the next.

Mix and Match

All of these factors will change for each situation, so you want a script that is workable and changeable no matter what the circumstances. In this way you can "mix and match" your components.

Some salespeople actually keep note cards that have the key points they want to get across for each product as well as the overall key points. They then put the cards in order of how they will make that individual presentation.

Don't hesitate to use note cards or an outline during the presentation. If it's to a group, they likely won't even notice. If it's to an individual, you can have a short script on a notepad in front of you. You can also use the notepad to jot down things the prospect says he or she is interested in.

CHAPTER 14

Efficient Prospecting

Your business can't grow if you don't get new customers. As a result, you will need to spend at least some time every week prospecting for new business. When it comes to sources for new customers, the sky is the limit, but be sure your efforts are cost-effective and not a waste of time.

Family and Friends

When most people get into network marketing, they choose their family and friends as their first prospective customers. That's natural—you know that your friends and family members are likely to trust you and will overlook little mistakes you might make during a sales call or meeting.

When you first start thinking about your prospective customers, make a list of everyone you know. Get out the mailing list from your last invitation-only event—even if it was your wedding twenty years ago—and copy down the names and phone numbers of everyone you invited.

SSENTIALS Plan to get at least 100 names on your first prospect list just by tallying up your list of family and friends. You might be surprised when you get a lot more. If you find your list is small, move on to acquaintances, too.

Next move on to the new people in your life. Add distant cousins, new friends, and everyone else you can think of. Call your mother and ask to borrow her address book. Call all your aunts and ask where all their kids are today. Find out where your ex-brother-in-law is living.

The First Message to Family and Friends

With your fledgling prospect list created, you now have to figure out the best way of contacting these people. The easiest approach should be to prepare a general letter that lets your loved ones know what you are doing and why you are excited about this opportunity, and to mail this letter along with a product catalog.

Each of these letters should be personalized. Try to add at least one paragraph that talks directly to the person, asking how his or her children are or alluding to an event you both attended. This is easily done with word processing and will make the letter seem much more personal.

You can also include a nice offer, like a 10 percent discount for family and friends or a bonus gift if they host a sales party. In a couple of weeks, you should follow up this mailing with a phone call.

Don't Overuse Your Relations

Family and friends will be invaluable to you when you start your business, but it's important not to abuse this group. Some new salespeople rely on their family and friends so much that eventually these people get resentful.

The best tactic is to ask them to buy the product and to keep them informed of special offers every month but then to back off for a while. If they are interested in the product, they will naturally order it because they won't have any reticence about calling you. If they are interested in becoming distributors, you will likely have some clues because they will start asking you questions at events such as family gatherings.

It's also important to remember that you have to keep living with these people or visiting them for special events. Because of that, you don't want to pressure them, especially to become distributors.

Don't risk family tensions by hard-selling your family. You may get the sale but lose out on your personal goals in the long run. If they don't buy from you today, they may change their minds once you are more successful.

Some network-marketing programs encourage you to sign up all of your family and friends as distributors, but don't fall into this trap. Not everyone has the same interests as you, and your friends and family members might feel pressured to join because they feel they owe it to you as a favor. Even if they are interested in network marketing, it might turn out that they are not very good at direct sales. If they don't live up to your or their own expectations, there could be hard feelings for years to come.

Friends of Friends

However, you can rely on your family and friends to use their contacts to build your prospect base. After all, they all have family and friends you don't know. These are the natural extension of your customer list.

Think of all their in-laws, school buddies, other friends, people they work with, and people they know through their hobbies and leisure activities. Eventually you will discover that every adult friend or family member you know is good for at least twenty new business contacts.

Sometimes you can simply ask people to give you a list of names. If you have already sold your friend or family member on the product, it's natural to say, "Who do you know that might like to buy this?" (It's also a good way to subtly plant the seed that this person might make a good distributor!)

FACTS

Every person you know can provide you with at least twenty new contacts. If you make the offer worth their while and they like your products, they will gladly provide those names.

If you're not comfortable asking for names directly, encourage your family and friends to have a sales party or to take extra brochures for these people. You might find some good customers this way without having to do any work at all.

The Message for Friends of Friends

When you're trying to turn friends of friends from prospects to customers, you already have a big advantage: the person who gave you their name.

As a result, you should use this name at least twice in your first contact with these people. If you write a letter, it should begin with, "Hi, I'm a friend of Joe Johnson's and he said I should contact you because you might be interested in. . . ." You might add another paragraph that says, "Joe was especially pleased with the XYZ product he bought from me, so I think you would be, too."

You also can give these people a special offer—"because you're a good friend of a good friend"—just as you offered your family and friends something special. Then follow up with a phone call within a couple of weeks.

Remember that the people who originally provided you with contact names are good friends of the people you are calling. They gave you the names because they felt they could trust you. Don't abuse that trust by trying to "hard sell" these contacts.

Think about Your Neighbors

Neighbors are in a class by themselves. They provide special opportunities but also special concerns.

You might not know your neighbor very well, but the fact that you live nearby makes this person a natural for selling to. Your neighbors could become your best customers just because you live so close and have at least one thing in common—your address.

However, neighbors sometimes like to keep their privacy and they might not want to be disturbed. They may not want to do business with you because they feel you are too close to them already. Likewise, they may feel that you are trying to take advantage of them because you live right next door.

Consider the ramifications if something goes wrong. Much like a family member, if you encourage a good neighbor to become a distributor and the situation doesn't work out, you could lose a good relationship.

Finally, think carefully before encouraging your neighbor to become a distributor for you. If he or she has a number of contacts that you can't reach, whether it's through family and friends or work relationships, that's great. However, if you live in a small community, you may find that you are competing directly with your neighbor for business.

Your Sponsor's Contacts

Your sponsor should have a number of ideas for getting new prospects. The good thing about these ideas is that they worked for your sponsor in the past and are likely to work for you.

Sometimes sponsors will start you off with a few of their own prospects that they have gleaned from sales parties or events such as county fairs. Your sponsor might also have a list of people he isn't comfortable selling to, including neighbors, family members, or even people at his full-time job. Having your sponsor's name as a reference when you get in touch with these people will make the sale easier.

Your sponsor might have ideas for obtaining names that she just hasn't gotten around to following up on yet or will be unable to do for one reason or another. A good example might be getting the list of people who are members of the Knights of Columbus. If the sponsor isn't a member and you are, that's an area in which you might collaborate. You could get the names, but since it was your sponsor's suggestion, you would share the list with her.

You might also find that if you brainstorm with your sponsor, together you will think of opportunities neither of you had previously considered. For example, maybe the sponsor likes to attend community fairs but can't cover all of them. You might offer to visit the ones she would have to miss. Or maybe your sponsor hadn't even considered asking his dad for his list of Vietnam Veterans Association members.

Schedule at least two hours a month to work on prospecting with your sponsor and some of your sponsor's other down-line members. Look for opportunities you couldn't do alone, such as manning a booth at the ten-day-long state fair. Also look for a chance to share prospect lists.

Other Members of the Down-Line

Just as your sponsor has good ideas for prospecting, you might find that others in your sponsor's down-line have had success in one area or another. Talk to them and find out what they recommend for getting prospect lists.

Also encourage your sponsor to develop a sharing attitude about prospects. For example, if someone has a prospect list and they've contacted the people on it several times, they should be willing to share the names of those who didn't respond. It's possible that a fresh contact with a different approach could land the business. Finally, by banding together you might find that you can get more contacts than you could alone.

The Power of Advertising

While many network marketers steer clear of advertising, there is definitely still a place for it under the right circumstances.

Advertising can be very cost-effective because it reaches many people for relatively little money. The problem, of course, is that those people must be motivated to then make a phone call to you. Motivating anyone to jump from interest in a product to actually placing the order can be extremely difficult with advertising alone.

The key is to be very selective when reviewing your advertising options and to consider whether money spent on a particular advertisement is really worth it. You might find that a single advertisement in a small market is worth more than many ads placed in a larger market.

FACTS

Print advertising can be very inexpensive if it reaches people who want your products. However, it can be a complete waste of money if the ad doesn't encourage people to take action.

Newspapers and Magazines

You probably don't want to advertise in a big-city paper, but what about your local community's weekly or monthly publication? Even big cities often have small weekly newspapers for local communities. Many communities also have weekly Shoppers that offer very inexpensive advertising.

Also don't forget about local magazines and newsletters. Church bulletins frequently have advertisers, for example, and the church's members are encouraged to support the advertisers. A club might ask for sponsors for its annual yearbook or other event. A community organization, such as the Jaycees, might ask for advertisers in its monthly newsletter.

In all cases, look at the cost of the advertisement as well as the audience it will be reaching. The most important question to consider is whether the readers of a particular newspaper, newsletter, or magazine would be interested in your products.

What to Advertise

Many people advertise the business opportunity of becoming a network-marketing distributor, but it may be more effective to advertise the items you are selling. If someone is looking to become a distributor they will call you anyway; advertising the business opportunity turns away everyone who might just want to give the product a try.

Many companies will provide print ad "slicks," ads in different sizes that are ready to be printed in the pages of a newspaper. If your company doesn't, don't worry. The information you need to include is very simple:

- The product name
- One or two key benefits of the product line
- Your name
- Your phone number
- An offer for free information or a free sample

Ask for More

Perhaps the most effective way to get your money out of advertising does not come from the actual ad. Instead, it comes from the free names you can get from the organization with which you place the ad.

For example, if you are supporting the Jaycees by buying an ad in their newsletter, tell them you would like a list of their members. They should be willing to provide you with at least last year's list of local members.

If you are running an advertisement in a local newspaper, ask if you can have a partial list of their subscribers, such as those who live in a certain area. Most will be reluctant to provide this at first but may offer compromises, such as a list of all the advertisers for the last year. (After all, behind every one of those businesses there's a person who may be interested in your products.)

Over the Airwaves

Radio can reach a lot of people for very little money. The problem is that it's even less influential than print because the person has to be listening closely and be willing to act on the information you present. If they don't have a pencil and paper handy, providing your phone number doesn't do a lot of good.

However, there are opportunities for making radio work as a prospecting tool. It's especially good to drive people to a special event. For example, you may tell people through a radio advertisement that you are exhibiting at the local county fair and anyone who mentions the radio ad will receive 10 percent off any order placed at the fair.

If you live in a small community with a local radio station, you could try placing an advertisement that encourages people to contact you directly. This works well, especially if most of the people in town know how to reach you. For example, maybe your wife is the only hairdresser in town. You could run an ad saying that people should stop by the hair salon and pick up a free coupon for 10 percent off the first order they place with you.

One concern about radio is that the announcer is often free to read your ad whenever she wants. You must specify in the contract that you want the ad read a certain number of times during certain hours of the day.

Don't Forget the Signs

And speaking of the hair salon, don't forget to put signs up in the salon that say you are selling this product line! In fact, have your brother put up a sign at the feed mill he owns and your sister put up a sign at her dress shop.

Signage of all sorts is a good method of attracting new customers. Put magnetic signs on your car doors and have a sign in front of your house that says you carry the product. Often people are looking to buy a product but don't know where they can get it. Or, in the case of well-known product lines, they remember how much they like the item once they see a sign.

Spread the Message Electronically

If you have chosen to align with a company that uses Internet sales as its main strategy, you will receive a great deal of training and software that helps you locate people based on their interests. For example, if you sell vitamins, it will pull out people who buy vitamins online.

Some companies will set up Web sites that offer people free items if they complete a survey. The answers to the survey, in turn, are used to tailor a message to the person to convince him to buy one or more of the company's products.

It's a good tactic that can work very well. However, these organizations are being watched very carefully because they can easily cross the line into spamming, sending out thousands of messages to people who didn't ask for the information.

Sending unsolicited e-mail, known as "spamming," is not only annoying—it's illegal. Only send personalized e-mail messages to people who have shown some interest in your products.

Ethical companies will encourage you to send many messages, but they will also ensure that the message headline tells people they are receiving this because of their interest in the product category. The message will also include information on how to respond if they do not want to receive more e-mails on the subject.

Other Ideas

Even if your company doesn't offer any special Internet services for you to take advantage of in your search for new customers, the World Wide Web still has many opportunities to offer. For example, you might list some of your items on a popular auction site such as eBay. While eBay doesn't allow you to offer to sell other products to a person as a result of their sale, you can tell the person you carry the full line of products and ask if they would be interested in getting a catalog.

You can also look for people who use the auction Web sites to buy items similar to the ones you are selling and then e-mail them with the chance to buy from you. Some recipients of these e-mails may find this tactic a bit unethical, but others will find it valuable. If someone complains, simply remove that person from your address list and do not contact him again.

Another method is to look at the e-mails you receive from your family and friends. Many people routinely copy thirty or forty people when they send a funny story or even family news. Simply take those names and send each of them a short e-mail message about your product line.

Finally, you may want to register your personal Web site with the many search engines so that anyone typing in your product or category name will be referred to your site.

Sending E-mail Messages

When you send someone an e-mail encouraging them to buy your products, your message must be extremely short. People don't have the attention span to read a lengthy message about you and your products. They likely clicked your e-mail open because they were curious (which means you did a good job writing an interesting subject title) and you have to turn that curiosity into action.

First, make sure that the title of your e-mail is not misleading—the product name might be enough—or the recipient will just get annoyed and delete the e-mail anyway. If it's a new item, try adding its main characteristic to the e-mail's title. Here are two examples: "All-Natural Cleaning Products" or "Kitchen Tools the Best Chefs Use."

In the body of the message, provide enough information to get the reader interested enough to visit your Web site or to e-mail you back with a request for a product brochure. If the product is new, mention its unique features in a few sentences. If it's a household-name product with a good reputation, offer a special to new customers.

Finding Distributors Online

While opinions differ, it can never hurt to start by using the product as the means of getting to know the person before encouraging him or her to become a distributor. You can always include brochures or other information about the sales opportunity with the order.

However, if you start by encouraging the sales opportunity you are missing the chance to build future distributors from the ground up and you definitely lose the chance to make product sales.

You can also take a more sophisticated route and create a Web site that is listed with major search engines under the key words "network marketing." This way, people who are specifically looking to become a distributor will find you when they are conducting a search online.

Mailing Lists

Mailing lists are one of the biggest businesses in this country. Every time a customer buys something from the Internet or a mail-order catalog, his or her name goes on a list that is sold to hundreds of other organizations. That's why you start receiving lots and lots of junk mail the second you subscribe to a magazine—direct-mail advertisers know that if you like the magazine, you might like their products, too.

If you have built a large sales organization, you can take advantage of national mailing lists to give to your distributors. A good example might be to get the subscription list for a health and fitness magazine if you sell vitamins and minerals. Usually these lists can be purchased in partial amounts by zip code.

If you are interested, simply look at a magazine you like and call the sales office listed somewhere on its masthead page—you will quickly reach the right person. (Truthfully, some magazines make more money selling these lists than they do on their actual advertising sales.)

You can also develop mailing lists on your own. Many network marketers display their products at county fairs, community events, and school functions. Some even buy space at a local shopping mall to sell product from a small cart. The reason isn't so much to sell as it is to gather names and addresses that you can then use to mail out catalogs and advertisements of special offers.

The Right Approach Is Key

Contacting people from a mailing list is the postal equivalent of a cold call—there is anonymity on both sides. You don't know whom you will reach and the recipient of your mailing is certainly not expecting to hear from you.

Consequently, your first sales message must be very quick and to the point. You might choose to send a postcard that is identical to your newspaper print ad or a short letter talking about the products and including a brochure, especially if the person willingly supplied his or her name.

You don't need to include anything personal about yourself and you certainly don't want to pretend you know what this person might want.

Current Customers

That's right! Each one of your current customers is a great resource for finding new customers. Just like your family and friends, your current customers represent a whole new world of contacts through their own families, friends, and acquaintances.

Remember that your current customers are prospects in their own right. They may become interested in buying more products from you and should always be considered prospects for your down-line.

You can gain contacts from these people in a number of different ways. The first is just to ask them for referrals. If they are happy with the products, they likely won't hesitate to give you a few names and phone numbers.

Current customers are such good sources of names that your company probably has several programs already set up for you to gather names from them. Product catalogs and sales brochures likely have a spot for people to provide the names of others who would be interested in the product.

Extra Encouragement for New Names

An easy method to expand your customer list is to encourage current customers to have sales parties where they can earn free products for themselves. Most companies have such programs in place if they have large product lines.

Distributors also often have "party months" where people who throw a party with a certain amount of sales get an extra bonus. If someone books a party at their party, they get another bonus. If someone from the party becomes a distributor, they get an even bigger bonus.

You can also do this without having a sales party. For example, simply tell each customer that you will give her 5 percent off the next order for every customer she supplies you with that orders more than $100 worth of products.

As an extra bonus for you, you might discover that someone's list of contacts is so good that it's worth encouraging them to become a distributor!

It's a Numbers Game

When you're prospecting, it's very easy to get discouraged. You know you have a great product so you think everyone you talk to or send a letter to will be excited as well. Unfortunately, you will quickly learn that people just aren't as responsive as you think they should be.

In many organizations, the salespeople are thrilled if just 1 out of every 100 prospects becomes a customer. That's a lot of paper, ink, stamps, and phone calls for just one sale.

As a result, the key is to target your prospects as carefully as you can. Don't waste money on people you are sure won't buy anything. If you're not sure whether they will buy, try a postcard with a special offer or a no-cost e-mail message. Save letters and time-consuming phone calls for people who have expressed at least some interest in the products.

Only a very small percentage of every prospect turns into a sale. And even fewer of those customers remain regulars. Your job is to weed out the nonsales prospects quickly so you don't spend precious time and money on them.

Finally, if you have contacted someone four times and nothing has happened, put them into a different prospect list that you contact just once a year. You can't afford the time or money to keep courting someone who won't respond.

Keep at It

Perhaps the most important thing to remember about prospecting is that it never ends. No matter how big your business becomes, you should still be looking for new customers and distributors.

Think of prospecting as a fun game. How many new people can you reach this month? How many can you turn into customers? Every new contact should be like a spark to your businessperson's brain, telling you that this one could be a big one.

CHAPTER 15

Basic Sales Skills

Not everyone responds to the same sales pitch. In fact, what convinces one person to buy will send the next one out the door empty-handed. Consequently, you need to know how to quickly identify personality types and modify your sales approach accordingly. This chapter will help you avoid sales pitfalls and perfect your sales technique.

It Takes All Kinds

Contrary to popular belief, there are all kinds of salespeople who sell in all kinds of ways. There is no one "sales personality." In fact, some of the world's most successful salespeople are low-key good listeners who just want to truly help someone.

**SSENTIALS** There are all different types of products and all different types of customers, and every sales situation is unique. Good salespeople will learn how to use their own style effectively with each particular item and customer. But first, they have to determine the way they like to sell.

Think about the experiences you have had with salespeople and you'll quickly see that they are not all the same. Chances are that you have encountered the four basic sales personality types in your daily life.

The Snake-Oil Salesperson

This person is fast-talking, doesn't let you get a word in edgewise, and has an answer for everything. He or she will claim that the product can do anything you want it to do—and then a little more.

To be fair, these people aren't always dishonest. They just like to talk and like to argue. They can be a lot of fun and frequently do well in areas such as time-share sales or collectibles.

The High-Pressure Tactician

This person also does a lot of talking but instead of telling you just how wonderful the product is, he or she will tell you that you must buy it. Sometimes the tactics are disguised in terms of creating an urgent need— this is the last one, interest rates are going up, and so forth—but the gist of the message is always that you would be an idiot not to buy it.

Again, to be fair, these people often know what they are talking about. There are often very good reasons for buying "right now." High-pressure tacticians make excellent stockbrokers and realtors.

The Super Soft-Sell Salesperson

Have you ever bought ladies' lingerie? If you have, you probably met this sales type somewhere along the way. She asks if you would like help and doesn't bother you beyond that. If you have a question, she will point you to the product that meets your needs and may try to sell you a little extra (massage oil or matching panties), but only if it really makes sense.

This salesperson can be deceptively successful. While she is acting as though she doesn't care what you buy, she actually is steering you toward the most expensive items and subtly encouraging you to trust her decision. And you do, of course, because you don't know a thing about her product line.

The Analytic Salesperson

This type of salesperson will present all sorts of numbers, showing you how scientific evidence supports her opinion that this is the right product for you. Insurance people are common to this group because they can point to numbers on both sides of the equation—your chance of needing the insurance given your unique situation as well as the savings you will reap if you buy the insurance.

While this type of salesperson can be extremely effective in most situations, they can also be infuriating if they sell items that are normally bought on impulse or if they are dealing with people who like to buy based on their feelings. Analytical salespeople frequently have the most trouble adapting their style to meet different selling situations.

Different Products Demand Different Styles

The problem, as you probably have discovered in your own life, is that sometimes you are looking for one type of salesperson and sometimes you are looking for another. For example, if a snake-oil salesperson tried to sell women's lingerie, she would try to convince you that just presenting this to your loved one would result in long-lasting affection. If a soft-sell person sold insurance, he would quickly have to look for another job. If the analytical type sold snake oil, she wouldn't have much to say.

Consequently, salespeople tend to gravitate to the type of product that works best for their particular style. Snake-oil salespeople like the thrill of the chase and never hope to make a repeat sale. Analytical types like the complex products. Soft-sell people like items that tend to sell themselves. Hard-sell people love to sell commodities because they can prove that they are the best salespeople.

QUESTIONS?

Do you know what your sales personality is?
If you know how you prefer to sell, you will be better able to adjust when the situation calls for a different type of sales strategy. You don't want to change yourself, just modify your presentation style a bit.

Luckily, network marketing frequently lends itself to a number of different sales styles. First, even a company with just one product actually has at least two products—the physical item that's being sold and the opportunity to be a distributor. A hard-sell approach can be necessary when the item is new, while a soft-sell works well when the product is a household-name brand. Then, because you must do much of the prospecting and marketing yourself, there is an element of analysis involved. So, whatever your natural sales style might be (and hopefully it isn't quite the caricature presented in these four examples) you will find a fit in network marketing.

Selling to Different Personalities

Just as different products require different sales tactics, so do different personality types. Some people are uncomfortable around high-pressure salespeople, while other people enjoy watching these salespeople perform. Some people must have all the scientific analysis before they buy even the most inexpensive item, while others buy because it makes them feel good. Some people buy because it helps others. Others buy because it makes them feel special.

It's hard to understand why someone thinks and behaves differently from you, but if you are going to succeed in sales, you have to accept the fact that they do and that they think their personality is the right way to be.

You will also have to learn quickly to identify the personality types and adjust your sales style accordingly. This doesn't mean that you should alter your personality and pretend you are someone you aren't; it just means that you will slightly change the information and the way you present it to make sure it best matches what the customer expects from a salesperson and what he or she needs to know about the product you are selling.

Many sales-training programs divide people into basic groups. For your purposes, you can try to group your customers into four categories.

Helpers

These people like to help other people. They tend to work in "helper" professions such as nursing, teaching, and social work. Their hobbies are frequently passive, such as gardening and needlework.

You'll recognize them because they talk about how much someone else needs them. They rarely brag, but if they do it's about how they helped someone.

Most people can mask their true personality pretty well until they are put into a stressful situation. Ask them how they reacted to something stressful in their lives recently, such as moving to a new home, losing a parent, or starting a new job.

Prima Donnas

These people like to be the center of attention. They have big egos and want to buy things because it makes them look like the big cheese. They tend to be self-employed or rather high up the corporate ladder. If they aren't successful at work, you will find them as the head of the PTA or the soccer team coach.

You'll recognize the prima donnas because they will talk about themselves—constantly. Ask them what they do for a living and an hour later you might get to ask another question.

Trendsetters

These people want to be the first on the block in everything they do—or buy. They are well read and often pay careful attention to gardening, home-decorating, and fashion magazines. However, they aren't always into fashion or the arts. Sometimes these people are trendsetters in one specific area, usually their hobby.

Trendsetters can have almost any job because their jobs aren't as important to them as the fact that they are trendsetters. They will live in the best neighborhood they can afford and drive a very expensive car. You will recognize the trendsetters because they will take you for a tour of their home and point out everything that's state-of-the-art.

Contemplators

These are the people who think and research and think some more before they buy something as simple as a bag of tea. They like to stick with the tried and true. They check consumer reports before they buy anything. A large number of them work with computers because their analytic skills are put to good use.

QUESTIONS?

What is your personality type?
It's important to know because it is your greatest liability. You will tend to think everyone buys for the same reasons you do and looks for the same things you do. It's better to assume that your customer is not at all like you and proceed from there.

You'll recognize the contemplators immediately because they like to analyze everything, including the ingredients in the chocolate-chip cookies you're serving.

Discovering the Reasons People Buy

As you've probably guessed, different personality types buy for different reasons. And yet, most people don't know that their personality is influencing how they make their purchases, especially when it comes to high-ticket items. In fact, they believe they need to be above such petty things as personality.

Interestingly, some people will even try to hide their true personality types in a sales situation. Prima donnas, for example, may pretend that they only care about the analytical side of the sale when, in fact, they desperately want the product because it will make them feel special. However, if you watch your customers' actions and listen to what they are (and aren't) saying, you will be able to detect their real personality.

Help for the Helpers

Helpers want products that will help them in their work and at home. They will react to words like "easy," "time-saving," and "effective." They are looking for comfort and probably don't care much about fashion or even scientific studies. Their motto is that if it works for them, it's the best thing on the market.

The helpers will probably react positively to any special missions your company might have. For example, if the company gives some of its profits to charity, the helpers will be impressed.

Although helpers will buy the first time to help you out, you should avoid sounding like you are making a plea in your presentation. You may make several sales because they feel sorry for you, but the relationship won't be sustained. In the end, the helpers who bought out of pity will be disappointed that you didn't "get better" with their help.

If you're trying to convince a helper to become a distributor, focus on the fact that this person could be bringing all those wonderful products to other people like them. After all, if they liked your product, wouldn't everyone they work with like it, too?

Impressing the Prima Donnas

Prima donnas will buy because they think other people will then think they are special. They want the high-end item and are willing to pay anything for it. They are looking for status symbols, not substance.

As a result, scientific analysis is lost on them. (Jaguars were selling well among high-income people even when they had the worst repair record of any car in the world.) They really don't care about helping people, unless it gives them a reason to brag. They may be interested in something new as long as celebrities are also using it. If a product is unknown, they want nothing to do with it, no matter how much of a bargain it is.

FACTS

When dealing with a prima donna, don't try to impose your idea of luxury on your customer. Instead, try to figure out what the customer sees as a status symbol. Look around the person's house and neighborhood to get clues as to what this person covets.

Prima donnas react well to testimonials from famous people. They like to hear that something is the best on the market (as long as you don't bore them with the details) and will respond well to words such as "high-end" and "luxurious."

Don't be fooled by the prima donna's income level. Many people who don't make much money believe more in the power of status symbols than do rich people. In fact, some of the poorest neighborhoods in the nation are studded with expensive clothing and jewelry.

To sell a prima donna into becoming a part of your down-line, you might like to emphasize what they will get when they achieve the top of the pyramid with the company. After all, a prima donna could hardly resist the luxury trips, vehicles, and other rewards that most stellar direct marketers earn.

Sell the Trend to the Trendsetters

Trendsetters want the newest items, but they only want them if they provide something new and different. For example, just because your line of kitchen cutlery is new, they won't necessarily be interested. However, if the knives are made out of the same alloy NASA uses on the space shuttle, they will definitely be interested.

Trendsetters are looking to be the first on their block to have something, so they will react well to news articles that talk about your product category becoming more popular. They will be interested to know that celebrities are using the product and will respond to words such as "new" and "state-of-the-art." Like prima donnas, trendsetters will only care that your product helps people if that has become trendy.

Interestingly, though, trendsetters really don't care about the item being a status symbol. In fact, many of them enjoy the fact that it sets them apart from their neighbors. They want the attention they get for being the first to have something.

If you're trying to convince a trendsetter to be a distributor, you better have a new product or be working for a company that continues to come out with new items. If your company tends to lag behind the times or does most of its marketing based on its "time-proven" products, you will have trouble selling the opportunity to these people.

Sell Value to the Contemplators

Contemplators want the best value for their money. They don't care if a particular product is a popular item, an expensive item, or a trendy item. They might take into account that it helps people in developing countries, but their driving force will be how good a value the product is.

That doesn't mean contemplators are looking for the cheapest item. On the contrary. They are very willing to pay for a top-end product if it means they have to buy it only once in their lives. They will also pay more if the product is guaranteed.

Contemplators will react well to products that have been around and have stood the tests of time. They will examine scientific studies carefully (so the ones you offer had better not have any flaws in them), and they will think about their purchase for weeks on end.

Unfortunately, contemplators don't easily change from the products they currently use, so they can be a tough sell. On the other hand, once you get them to change, you will probably keep these customers for life.

If you're trying to convince a contemplator to become a distributor, first make sure your product lends itself to this person's scrutiny. Then, present all the data that show the value the products offer as well as the value in becoming a distributor. If the argument is valid, the contemplator will eventually make the right choice.

Contemplators know all the sales tricks. They will call you on every statement you make and every piece of data you provide. If you are selling to a contemplator, you must be prepared with your facts because there is no room for error.

And What about the Bargain Hunters?

Bargain hunters can be found in all four groups, but the needs of true bargain hunters are different. For example, a contemplator will look for the best value for the money. A helper likes to find a great bargain so that the money saved may be used for a good cause, such as helping a nephew pay for college. A trendsetter will be thrilled to have the bargain as long as the item is trendy, and will be proud that he or she found it for the least money. And a prima donna will appreciate the discount as long as no one finds out about it!

Finding and Fulfilling a Need

The key with all these groups is to find out what they truly need in their lives, and that won't necessarily mirror their personality type. For example, just because you are selling a cool new skin cream it doesn't mean every single trendsetter will want to purchase it. Our personalities are merely the backdrop for our needs.

To discover what people need, you need to delve into their lives. Ask questions and find out what they need help with. It's very likely that something happening in the person's life will be a trigger to sell the product.

Once you have introduced yourself, start to ask about their job, their family, and their hobbies:

- Do they like their job?
- Is it stressful?
- Are their kids in day care?
- Are they in athletics?
- How are the kids doing in school?
- What do they do for fun?
- How did they get involved in their hobby?
- Is their hobby time-consuming?
- Is it expensive?
- Why do they like it?

Then pay attention to all the answers you get. It is likely that you will find a few areas in which the person isn't totally satisfied. Those are your clues to determining their needs. Focus on those areas of dissatisfaction and see if there is any way you can make your product help the person meet this need, even if the person doesn't yet know they have the need!

One Product, Different Strategies

Let's use an all-natural skin cream as an example.

You find out that the helper is a nurse who likes to do needlepoint. She has two children of her own and is sponsoring a poor child in a developing country. Her hands get chapped from her nursing duties but she has plenty of skin creams and knows all about them. Yours is just another product that contains aloe and other natural ingredients that are gathered in the rain forest. It's not any cheaper or any better than what she currently uses.

However, she may be intrigued by the fact that your company works with the native people to harvest the plants used in the creams, thus supplying a living wage to a community in a depressed part of the world. Your product matches up with the best creams on the market *and* it meets your customer's need to help people on the other side of the planet.

Or let's say you are selling to a prima donna. Your product is the latest and greatest. It's been written up in all the magazines. That's intriguing to the prima donna, but it's not enough—it doesn't really make her stand out in a crowd because no one really knows that she's wearing a particular hand lotion.

As you talk to her, you find out that she has just moved into a new house and is new to the neighborhood. You could suggest that the prima donna hold a sales party so that she can show all of her neighbors that she was the first on the block to find out about your product line—and show off all the luxury items in her new house.

Then, you try selling the same cream to a trendsetter. This particular customer has told you that she just purchased a skin cream used by Madonna and Brad Pitt. It's flown in weekly from Paris, where it is handmade in small batches.

Whew, it's hard to compete with that. But wait, you find out that she has a three-month-old baby who is having trouble with diaper rash. You drag out your articles that show how all the common diaper rash products contain preservatives and man-made chemicals. Your product, on the other hand, is all-natural and has been proven to work on diaper rash. You encourage her to follow the popular trend of using only natural items on a baby's skin, and she decides it is worth a try.

FACTS

If you can fulfill a person's need by relating it to his or her personality style, you will have no trouble making the sale. Use cues you receive from casual conversation to decipher what need your product might fulfill.

And what about the contemplator? One particular customer has looked at all the hand lotions out there and decided that yours isn't any better than the one she currently uses. When you talk to her longer, however, you find out that her mother is going through radiation treatments for breast cancer. You point out that because your product is all-natural, it doesn't aggravate the radiation burns and helps soothe the dry skin.

The contemplator has been wondering how to reduce her mother's pain and anxiety because it's causing her to lose valuable work time. Your news clippings show that aloe is the best product to relieve radiation burns. Yes, she might be able to search out another item that might be a few cents cheaper, but she needs something today and you have what she needs. Your availability provides the extra value she needs.

Changing Your Style

You will need to have a distinct selling style for each of your customers, depending on their personality types. That means that occasionally you may have to tone down your natural style and become better versed in areas that make you a bit uncomfortable at first. You don't have to stop being who you are. You just have to care about the other person's need to have their personality style take precedence.

Helpers will want a soft sell. They will want to hear about your reasons for selling the product. Going through the brochure over a cup of herbal tea is a good idea. If you're presenting to a group, keep your style slower and softer. Give them ample time to touch the products. Don't overwhelm them with details.

Prima donnas like the flamboyant sell. Do you have a computer presentation? All the better. Suggest this customer host a party. Expect to be outgoing and energetic when you talk to this person. If you have expensive clothing and jewelry, wear it to these sales meetings.

QUESTIONS?

I'm naturally a soft-sell person. How can I possibly sell to someone who wants energy and flamboyance?
You don't have to be extremely extroverted yourself. Just provide some glitz in your presentation and be enthusiastic about your product.

Trendsetters can be either introverted or extroverted. If your customer is extroverted, bring out your energetic, talkative style. If he or she is introverted, become soft-spoken and gentle. The important thing is to make it clear how your products are new and different. The trendsetters will look for evidence that your product is on a trendy upswing—they won't just take your word for it. Be prepared with the answers and you'll have an easy sale.

Contemplators want the data. They will need to see comparison charts about product performance as well as price comparisons. They will question every claim you make, so you better have proof. Most contemplators prefer a more low-key presentation. After all, scientists are rarely live-wires.

Overcoming Objections

Objections are a natural part of the selling and buying process. It sometimes seems that people are trained to make objections because they are afraid to be overly eager to purchase something.

In some cases, people like to throw up objections just to see if you can keep your cool while they are making your life difficult. In other cases, people have real qualms that you have to learn to overcome.

FACTS

Objections are a fact of life in the sales world. Don't take them too seriously or feel as though you have failed if you can't overcome every objection thrown at you. Some objections are just meant to be a polite way to say no.

Be wary when dealing with objections, though. Sometimes people just want to say something to make you go away. For some reason you haven't discovered the need that will make them buy your product. Or maybe your product truly isn't a good fit for them. Whatever the reason, if they continue to object after you have resolved the first few objections, you are better off leaving for the moment. You can always give them a call in a few weeks or even months.

Product-Oriented Objections

Here are some basic ways to overcome common objections to purchasing the product:

- *It costs too much.* Compare it to the cost per dose. Also compare it to products of similar quality.
- *I don't buy anything I can't see.* Offer to take the product back if they don't like it or to buy the product yourself and let them use it.
- *I already have enough of that kind of stuff.* Point out how this is better than what they currently use.
- *I'm broke.* Ask them not to spend more money this month, but to buy something from you that they normally would buy from the store.
- *I never buy from door-to-door salespeople.* Explain that you don't sell door-to-door, you sell directly to customers. You don't knock on doors unless you know the people are interested.

Objections to Becoming a Distributor

Here are some basic ways to overcome common objections to getting involved in network marketing as a distributor:

- *I don't have the time.* Provide a list of what they can achieve if they give the business just one hour a day.
- *I'm just not a salesperson.* Everyone is a salesperson. You just have to find your style and your niche. Give them a copy of this book.
- *People think network marketing is a scheme.* Ask, "Then why have so many companies used it successfully for so many years?" Give them a copy of this book.
- *I'm shy.* Tell them that shy people make the best salespeople because people wouldn't think that they were trying to pressure them into anything.
- *I'd like to, but my spouse would be angry.* Have your spouse talk to their spouse.
- *I'm not smart enough; it's too complicated.* List all of the training and materials that the company provides.

CHAPTER 16
Getting Out There

The key to successful network marketing is dealing with people. There are many different ways of meeting people in a situation conducive to selling. And whether it's a one-on-one sales call or a large sales party, you will need specific skills to convince people to buy your products and to become part of your down-line.

The Sales Meeting

Some companies sponsor events that are open to the public. At these events, they talk about their products and encourage people to become distributors. Sales meetings are relatively glamorous, held in nice hotel ballrooms with a nice selection of hors d'oeuvres being served.

These events invariably attract people who are "just curious." Sometimes you find that guests at the hotel are just popping in to see what's going on. As a result, the sales meeting can be a good place to make sales. If you can connect with people and befriend them, it's likely that you will get their business.

This initial bond can be an important component of eventually becoming a sponsor. They will remember that you were the person who "rescued" them from a room of strangers.

Sales-Meeting Skills

When you're at the meeting, you want to keep yourself open to new people. Don't start talking to people you already know. Instead, go up to people who seem to be lost in a corner, looking bewildered.

Try to connect with at least three "lost" people before the actual presentation begins. Ask why they are there, but don't start talking about the product unless they ask you questions. Be curious about them, friendly, and helpful in providing information about the company and the products, but don't try to talk them into anything.

If they say they are interested in becoming a distributor, talk about your love for the job, but don't push. Keep in mind that these people are just looking for a little more information and want to get it in a nonthreatening environment.

Making the Sale

After the presentation, search out the people you connected with before. Chances are, you're sitting at a table with at least one of them. Ask what they thought of the presentation, the company, the products, and the opportunity. Do they think it looks like something that might interest them?

More than likely your newfound friends won't sign up to be distributors right away. However, he or she may be interested in buying something. And guess what? You're right there to take the order!

In later months this person could very likely become a distributor. In the meantime, you will have built a bond with this customer because you rescued him or her from a roomful of strangers. It's just natural that you will become this person's sponsor.

The Sales Party

Sales parties are common in many network-marketing programs because they are so successful. You can make one presentation to anywhere from three to thirty people. Because they know the host, every one of those thirty people will buy something, giving you the opportunity to make more sales via more parties.

It also frequently provides more loyal customers. At first, the attendees make purchases because they want to help out the host— after all, they are well aware that the host receives free products from you just for holding the event. With that in mind, they buy a little more than they might if you approached them as individuals. The more items they try, the more they like, and the more they reorder again and again.

Do not try to make detailed presentations about your company at a sales party. People are there to visit as well as to buy. Keep the environment light and fun, or you will lose potential sales.

In addition, a sales party presents an excellent opportunity to prospect for new distributors. People who might be considering network marketing have a firsthand look at how easy it is to sell these products, and they feel as though it's safe to ask you questions because you can't get too high-pressure with several other people in the room.

Not All Products Like to Party

If other distributors who work for your network-marketing company host sales parties, you know that your products lend themselves to such selling opportunities. Chances are, your sponsor will encourage you to host sales parties and will already have taken you to several where he gave the presentation.

However, if you have a new product and you're not sure if it lends itself to a sales party, there are ways to discover if this is a good sales tactic for you.

First, realize that you need to be able to keep the group interested for at least half an hour. You probably can't satisfy everyone with just one or two different items, no matter how excited you are and how much you can talk about them. A good rule of thumb is to avoid sales parties if your product line doesn't contain at least twelve different products at different price points.

You will have different personalities attending and everyone will have different needs, so your product line should have at least a dozen different elements in a variety of price ranges—and ideally a couple hundred—if you are going to make sales parties work for you.

A Thousand Ways to Party

Today's sales parties take all forms. Tupperware, for example, encourages working women to have "book" parties, where they just take a bunch of books to their coworkers and let people order at their leisure. Some companies have book "showers," where everyone gathers to buy stuff for a new bride or a new mother.

As you think about parties, try to break out of the box. One Tupperware salesperson, for example, gave her business a big boost when she started doing parties for her brother's gay friends. No one had ever sold to them as homemakers before. She had several months of parties booked from just one event.

Other people have tried hosting parties with college students, new mothers, or other groups that all have something in common. Think about your life and what groups you know of that may be in need of your products but have yet to be introduced to them. Encourage someone from that group to be your first host.

Look for unusual groups of people to gather together for parties. In today's two-income families, many people are too busy to build the relationships that spur parties, so you could actually be doing people a favor by bringing your product to them in this setting.

What to Do with a Party

Parties are a wonderful way for a new distributor to build business, because they tend to take on a life of their own. Chances are, at least one person at the party has tried your products. He or she usually starts chiming in during your presentation, taking some of the pressure off of you to come up with witty remarks and insightful thoughts about your products.

Before a party, be sure to research the guests. Ask the hostess about the people.

- Will they be male, female, or a mixed group?
- What age groups will be represented?
- Will most people be married or single?
- Do they live in the city, the suburbs, or the country?
- How much education do most of them have?
- Is it likely that they have heard of the product before?
- How does the host or hostess know these people?

These facts will help you tailor your presentation to the group. You might decide not to cover some products because the group wouldn't be interested in them, and instead concentrate on those that will require more attention because they are most appropriate for this group.

Not researching the group can lead to disastrous consequences. One distributor for a line of kitchen items who didn't do her research beforehand wanted to make a presentation that would entice the guests to join her down-line. Her strategy was to ask the attendees what they would do with an extra $100 a month. All of the women looked at each other and rolled their eyes. They lived in an affluent suburb and some of them made more than $100,000 a year. They didn't need $100, although there might have been other tactics that could have convinced them to become distributors.

Identify Potential Distributors Before the Party

If you are good friends with the hostess, before the party ask her to identify anyone who might be a good candidate for becoming a sponsor. Ask the hostess to think of people who want to make a job change, housewives, people looking for a lifestyle change, or anyone else who might be a good candidate.

Then, try to spend a little extra time with these people after the formal presentation is over. Don't come right out and say that the hostess thinks they'd be a good at distributing. Just go up to them and begin a casual conversation that highlights the opportunities of network marketing.

Those who are good candidates will get interested and will ask you questions. You can follow up with them in a few days to ask if they have more questions.

The Presentation

Because your sales-party presentation is directed at a group of people with different personalities, try to give a good solid presentation that is enthusiastic but not too high-energy. At these parties, people are in the mood to listen and even learn. They don't want to feel drained after watching you pour out all your energy.

Watch the group carefully as you begin talking about a product. If they don't seem interested, cut that part of your presentation short and go on to the next item. If one person is interested, he or she can ask you questions after the presentation is over.

Also be sure to include some demonstrations. If possible, show your products in action. If that isn't possible, be sure to handle the items and pass them around so people feel involved and have something more than just your spoken presentation from which to form an opinion about your products.

FACTS

Always have enough "material" in your presentation repertoire to give a presentation twice as long as you plan, because you may discover that you have to change your plans significantly when you meet the attendees.

You likely won't be able to answer everyone's questions, so it's nice to have handouts that talk about the technical details of a product or the details of being a distributor. That saves you from having to spend all your time with one very interested person.

Try to get the attendees involved by playing a few games or at least asking questions during the party. This will make you seem more like a friend to them and will put them in a better frame of mind for purchasing.

Don't have a presentation that is longer than one hour, and make sure you allow enough time at the end of the party for people to chat with each other, ask you questions, and fill out their orders. Let people enjoy the party atmosphere as they learn about your products.

The Conference

Any event that brings a large number of strangers to you may be called a conference—county fairs, small-business fairs, community get-togethers, and even school functions can all be included under this heading. Because conferences bring together a lot of people, they are an excellent way to gain new prospects and customers.

Any such large event requires a booth or a table where you can set up a few samples of your products and some brochures. As people come by, you can answer their questions about the items, make demonstrations, and possibly even take orders.

Conferences inevitably get a bad reputation because people feel they aren't worth the time and money. They sit at a booth or table all day and not much happens. Maybe they give out free stuff or take down names, but they don't see much money coming in.

However, it's all a matter of attitude. If you realize that a conference is a cornerstone event for your business, it takes on a whole new light. You are not at the conference to make money. You are at the conference to set the stage for making money.

Gather Names

The key role of a conference is to gather names. You want to get as many as you can, so you need something that will entice people to provide their names, phone numbers, addresses, and even e-mails. Here are a few suggestions for soliciting this information:

- Give people a small sample of your product in exchange for filling out small forms with their names and addresses.
- Have a drawing for $25 in free product. Be sure the raffle tickets have room for all the pertinent information.
- Play a game for free products. When the person hands you a completed form, you hand them a dart to throw at balloons that have product numbers behind them, or they get a chance to pick a numbered ducky from a fish bowl.
- Offer something free to everyone at a later date. Mary Kay, for example, offers free facials to everyone who signs up at a booth. Every one of those names goes to a distributor who then calls the person and sets up the appointment.
- Sell something necessary. In the summer, many distributors will sell lip balm, sun visors, or water bottles. As they collect the money, they get the buyer's pertinent information.

The Right Space

In order to attract visitors, you must have an enticing booth. Think exciting, colorful, and high-energy, and plan what you will do with every square inch of space you have been allotted.

Start with the backdrop. You will likely have some kind of a curtain or wall behind you. You need a big, easily read sign that tells people what your products are and what company you represent. If the conference organizer insists that you use the little black-and-white sign they provide, fine, but move it off to the side and put your big, colorful sign right in the middle of your space just above a standing adult's eye level.

The backdrop is also a good place to hang posters, pictures of products being made or used, or anything else that hangs flat. You could also hang product samples here.

Next, consider your table space. Be sure to cover it with a nice tablecloth, add a small display with products, some brochures, and a place to collect names and addresses. Also add some "softening" elements such as a potted plant. You want the space to appear friendly, not harsh and sterile.

You are competing with hundreds of other exhibitors for the attendees' time and attention at a conference. As a result, your display must be eye-catching and exciting while offering the attendee a reason to linger.

Also consider moving your table to the side so people can actually enter your booth space. This is more intimate and gets people more actively involved with you and your products. If this is possible, consider bringing or renting a carpet remnant to further soften the space.

Finally, look to add other displays. Can you bring in a nice literature rack to hold your product brochures? Can you add tables along the sides? Do you have any large products that could be set up for display?

Working the Conference

Conferences can be very wearing. Any time you spend eight or more hours a day on your feet talking to people, you get very tired. It works very well if you can share the event with at least one other distributor. If not, try to convince family members to take a few shifts for you.

People don't like hard-sell salespeople when they are attending conferences, so you should be friendly but stay in the background until someone asks you a question. Greet everyone and be careful not to spend too much time talking to friends or family members who might stop by.

Sit down as rarely as possible. You want to stay on eye level with the people coming by. In addition, if you sit down you give the impression that your products and your sales message are boring.

Dress nicely. If it's a county fair on a hot day, you don't need to be in a suit, but nice slacks and a polo shirt are always preferable to blue jeans or shorts and T-shirts. Remember that you are showing people what it's like to be a distributor, so your first impression is very important.

Interact with the Product

Samples and demonstrations are perfect for conferences. They will draw people to your space no matter where you are located and will keep them there longer than they would otherwise stay. Samples have the added benefit of getting someone to like your product without having to sell it to them.

Try thinking of unique ways to demonstrate your products. Can you give ongoing demonstrations, such as the ever-popular eyeglass cleaner demonstration salespeople do at county fairs? If your product is complicated, such as a ladder that folds away into one square foot of space, can you schedule demonstrations every half hour? One company that sells cleaning supplies has a simple demonstration in which its soap and a popular consumer brand are each mixed with water in covered jars. People can shake the jars and see how much "filler" is in the consumer brand.

In addition, be sure to have enough products on hand that you can sell to people who are interested. There is nothing more frustrating than wanting the product today and seeing it on the table but not being able to get it.

The One-on-One Sale

The one-on-one sale is a common strategy in many network-marketing programs that require an in-depth discussion to close the sale, but the problem with this method is its inefficiency. You can spend an hour selling to just one person and can end up making just a few pennies.

Your product is right for the one-on-one sale if the typical individual sale makes you at least $100. Your company will likely have elaborate sales scripts for you and training on how to handle typical objections.

SSENTIALS

If you and your product line are oriented to one-on-one sales, you will probably make your first contacts by phone and try to set up times to visit with your prospects. Furthermore, one of your major concerns will be to get a large number of prospects to follow up with.

Start with a Phone Call

Before you attend a one-on-one sales meeting, you will have set it up first; most often, you can do that by phone. When you call, start off by telling the person why you are calling and how you got his or her phone number.

Then, don't waste the person's time. Simply ask if he would be interested in learning more about your products. Tell him that you will take no more than an hour of his time and you can do it at any time and place that's convenient for him. If your prospect list is good, a fair number of people will grant you an hour of their free time and agree to meet with you.

If the prospect says no, don't write her off just yet. Ask if you can send her more information, and contact her again in a few months.

Analyze the Prospect

Remember, the potential sale must be worth the effort of a one-on-one meeting. Think about your prospect. Will this person be able to afford your high-end product?

Does this person have many contacts who would be good customers? In this case, you may want to work on the individual sale in hopes that the person will later have a party or at least give you a list of names to contact.

Also analyze the prospective customer's personality and plan a strategy for gaining the most from the time you spend. The one-on-one sales meeting is the perfect opportunity to fine-tune a sales presentation to the customer's individual needs.

Begin by listing all the details you know about this prospect: How you got his name and other facts—that he works with your sister or that he lives in a wealthy neighborhood, for example. If this prospect is a friend of a friend, call your initial contact and find out all you can about the person and what his needs may be.

Make the Last Preparations

The day before your meeting, you should call to confirm the time and place. At that point, you can ask your prospect a few questions to help determine her personality type. Find out about her work, hobbies, and family.

Finally, pick out just three interesting points you want to discuss based on your best guess about this person's personality. You should be well-versed in all aspects of your product in case the prospect wants to go on to other topics, but you should plan to concentrate on just a couple of key areas. After all, it takes just one reason for the prospect to become a customer.

Solicit Distributors

The one-on-one meeting is perhaps the best way to turn a customer into a distributor. You may first meet a potential distributor during a sales conference or sales party, but you almost certainly will "close the deal" in a one-on-one meeting.

This sales strategy begins just as the one to sell products. You begin with a phone call to set up the meeting. You probably sell product the first time but, because you have analyzed the person well, you judge that he or she is a good candidate for becoming a distributor. Over the course of several visits, you can begin building a close relationship with this person; eventually, you can start subtly shifting the conversations away from products and on to the company.

Making Cold Calls

We don't do too many cold calls on a door-to-door basis anymore, although they aren't a bad idea, especially if you have an item that is new to a geographic area. In this case, it's best to have some small samples to give away along with brochures. Don't be a pest. Introduce yourself, tell them what you're selling, and ask if you can leave a sample. Then call back in a few weeks.

It's more often that your sales call just seems like a cold call. Maybe you've met the person once at another customer's party. Or maybe you got their name from the list you gathered at the county fair. They're not exactly cold prospects, but they surely aren't hot prospects either.

In these cases, you have a nice opportunity to mention how you got their name, then to make them an offer, such as a free product or 10 percent off their first purchase. You have a reason for calling or sending them a letter, and they aren't totally caught off guard by your approach.

Use the Phone

As with the one-on-one meeting, cold or semicold calls invariably start with a phone call. You will introduce yourself and tell why you are calling. Try to mention how you got the person's name as quickly as you can.

QUESTIONS?

I'm terrified of picking up the phone to make a cold call. What can I do?
Always have a reason to call. For example, tell the person you are calling because you got her name from a friend or remind her that she stopped by your booth at the fair. Save the real cold calls for when you have more experience.

If your product is simple to sell, you might go into a short sales presentation right there. Explain the benefits of the item and ask for the order. However, it's more likely that the person will want you to send him a product brochure or other information.

If that's the case, be sure to send the information along with a personal note about the telephone conversation and how you think this product would be a good fit for his needs or interests.

Follow Up

Then follow up with the person about a week after you have mailed the information. Find out whether he is interested in ordering anything. If he seems unwilling to order, ask if he has any questions. If he does, answer them. If he doesn't, give him an enticing offer, such as 50 percent off any one product for a new customer. If he still isn't interested, ask if you can call back in a few weeks.

Always follow up a mailing within a week to make sure the person knows you are still interested in her. Nothing can kill a sale faster than letting a contact grow cold, so don't forget to make that phone call!

E-mail Sales

E-mail is a wonderful method of selling, especially after you've established a customer base. You can use it to solicit sales much as you would over the phone. The benefit is that you don't catch people while they are having dinner or are too busy to talk, because they can read the e-mail at their leisure.

E-mail is especially effective if you have a Web site where customers can place orders. In this case, you can e-mail them and simply tell them about your Web site. Then you can send out monthly e-mails with product specials or tips for using them.

Keep your messages short and to the point—three sentences should be enough to introduce the product. You can have a longer message if you want to list several different items that are on sale.

CHAPTER 17

Customer Relationship Management

In the world of big business, retaining customers is known as "customer relationship management," and working to ensure that you keep customers happy and coming back for more sales is very important—the best customers are those who are loyal to you and your products.

Setting Up a Database

You should have a file on every customer you have ever sold to, even if it was just one small sales transaction that took place several years ago. It's easy to keep these types of records electronically, especially if you know how to set up a database with Access, Excel, or any other software program, because the files can be updated quickly. However, if you don't have a computer or don't find it reliable, keeping a paper file works just as well.

These files should be very accessible to you, because you will be working with them more and more as your business grows. You should make a point of updating them every month or even every week.

FACTS

Databases are the lifeblood of a business's marketing strategy. They help ensure that you get the right message to the right people with the least amount of time and money.

Creating a Filing System

If you choose to create a paper filing system, make a separate file for each customer and label it with her name and the date she made the first purchase. At first, it may seem silly to have so many nearly empty file folders in your file cabinet, but you will find that over the course of several years, the individual files can become very large.

Divide all the files into three distinct groups based on the date each customer last purchased from you. Keep the files on people who have ordered within the last three months in the front of your file drawer, those who have ordered within the last year in the middle, and those who ordered more than a year ago in the back.

Within each of these groups, the individual file folders should be organized alphabetically. Use a different colored label for each of the three groups of customers. That way, when it comes time to refile the customer's folder, you know exactly where it should go. When the person changes groups, you can easily paste a new label over the old one.

Electronic Databases

You can organize your electronic database in the same way. Most will allow you to alphabetize by a particular entry (such as the last name); you can also search for files in a number of ways, such as by name, by the last entry you made, or by the date you last updated the file.

You can also find programs that will search for key words, such as a product name. In that way you could call up a list of people who purchased one of your products, perhaps to alert them to a new line of products in that area.

If you choose to keep your database on a computer, be sure to download it to a floppy disk or CD-ROM every time you update it. The database is the lifeblood of your business; you can't risk losing it if your computer crashes.

Essential Data

Whatever your filing system, your records should include three types of data: essential, active, and passive (see Appendix B for a sample customer information form). Essential data is the contact information that you need to do business with the person:

- Name
- Address
- Phone numbers
- E-mail address

You can obtain some of this information without ever talking to the customer—it might come from any number of sources. Because you keep records of all your prospects, you should already have this information on each customer's prospect information form. When a prospect becomes a customer, all you need to do is transfer that information into a new-customer entry.

Active Data

The next set of information in your database, active data, records every interaction you have ever had with this customer.

In particular, you need to keep track of the date you first made contact with the customer and how it was made—with a phone call, by mail, at a party, and so on. Make a note if you were referred to this customer by your friend, family member, or another customer.

Make sure you also add any information that might help you in future sales calls with the customer. For example, did the customer say she had tried the products in the past and liked them? Did she say that her uncle was a distributor for the same company in Colorado? Did she say she had read about your company in a newspaper article?

The next piece of active data is a list of everything the person ever purchased from you and the dates he or she purchases the items. This is done so that at any given time you know what the person has tried—and has not tried—within your product line.

At a glance, you will then be able to see if she has stopped purchasing one item and started purchasing another. You will be able to see if she has cut down on her purchases recently or if they have increased. You then can use this information to make a sales call on the person. Find out what's happening in her life that spurred the change, then use that new information to sell more products to her.

Keep your customer database information as secure as possible. You don't want your teenagers to discover information about their friends' parents, for example, and you certainly don't want a customer to find out that you have put him into a "buying group."

Next, record every interaction you have with this customer. List all of the mailings you send and the date you sent them. List phone calls and what you talked about. If you had to solve a problem, such as an incorrect order, list the date of the conversation and how you resolved the issue.

Likewise, if the person ever makes a comment that leads you to believe he or she might like to be a distributor, make a note of that. This includes comments about liking the product a lot, envying your lifestyle, or wanting to make a change in their job.

Passive Data

Passive data is information you glean by talking to the customer or observing him; typical passive data are:

- Marital status
- Approximate age
- Number of children and approximate ages
- Signals of buying power (such as expensive jewelry, furniture, or cars)
- What the customer and/or spouse does for a living
- What type of community they live in
- Their hobbies

SSENTIALS You can scan passive data periodically to determine if there are areas that you can use to increase the customer's purchases. For example, you may note that your customer is pregnant and will be ready for a certain line of products in a couple of months.

Categorizing Your Customers

The purpose of all this information is to classify your customers into distinct groups so you can apply specific marketing strategies to each. You already know that each type of customer needs a different message. Now you can group these people together to make your marketing efforts easier.

Note that this is different from the sales tactics you use on the individual customers. The database information has very little to do with the customer's unique personality. Instead, it provides real information on where the customer is in his or her life. That information, in turn, helps you decide which products to suggest to the customer. You still have to tailor the exact sales message to the customer's personality.

Group 1: The Future Affiliates

This group includes customers who you feel are good prospects for becoming distributors. You will want to stay in constant contact with them, perhaps phoning them every few weeks, to see if they still like the products you are selling and to drop hints about how great it is to be a distributor.

Even if they haven't voiced their interest, these people may be interested in a few years, so if you think they're worth pursuing, they're worth keeping on the Group 1 list.

Group 2: The Enthusiasts

This group includes all the customers who buy a lot of products from you. They love what you are selling and eagerly buy new items when they come out. Pick a dollar amount that signals a "good customer," such as $100 a month, and put everyone who spends that much on your products on the Group 2 list.

You also need to maintain frequent contact with these people in order to keep them updated on the specials and the new items that are available. Invite them to special sales events at your home, wine and dine them when you can, and send them a new brochure every time you get one—and follow up each one of these mailings with a phone call.

Group 3: The Loyalists

Group 3 are the loyal customers. Although they aren't big spenders, like the enthusiasts, they do make regular purchases. In network marketing, they are the meat and potatoes of your business, the people you can't live without.

Keep in touch with these people, but don't overburden them. Send them your monthly mailings and make an occasional phone call—just to check in. Periodically, you can try to mail them personal letters or postcards to try to "bump them up" into the enthusiasts group. Let them know about new products and offer special sales that encourage them to try items they haven't yet purchased.

Group 4: The Laggards

These people hardly ever buy from you. They might have placed one purchase at a party, but after repeated mailings and phone calls you can't get them to buy again. In the best of cases, they make a very occasional purchase—perhaps once or twice a year.

Pay careful attention to the "laggards" list, because you may find that it isn't worth your time and money to continue contacting many of these customers. Or you may decide that these people are worth just one mailing every few months.

While you may decide to ignore many of the people on this list for long periods of time, they are also a source of very good prospects. After all, every one of them has at least tried the product, so you don't have to spend a great deal of time educating them. You just have to find a better approach to selling to them.

Other Ways of Categorizing Customers

You can also categorize your customers based on their demographics. For example, you will naturally divide your list into people with a great deal of purchasing power and those with less disposable income. You might divide them by age or sex, if that is applicable to your product line. Another common grouping is by marital status and whether they have children.

Many times you identify these groups as you are perusing your files on a rainy day. Suddenly you notice that ten or even twenty files all have something in common. You start to wonder if that commonality could be the basis for a specific marketing message. And off you go.

Other times you will be searching for specific things. For example, if your company is coming out with a new line of products for teenagers, naturally you will scan all your files—even the laggards—for people with teens.

Common Activities

One strategy that frequently reaps big rewards for network marketers is to look at people's hobbies. If your company carries a wide range of products—no matter what they are—chances are the people's hobbies will in some way attract them to specific items. For example, if you carry a product line that has items applicable to gardening, you might want to figure out how many of your customers are ardent horticulturalists.

Or let's say you carry a line of women's makeup and you find that a number of your customers are into ballroom dancing. Does your makeup hold up well during physical activity and stress? This group of customers might appreciate knowing that in fact it does.

QUESTIONS?

What use is all this categorizing if I have just one or two products I sell?
In that case, you can highlight specific product benefits based on a group's specific needs. Low-cost, made in the U.S.A., high-quality, all-natural, easy-to-use, and other benefits all appeal to different groups of people.

Common Jobs

Another way to categorize your database is by occupation. For example, perhaps you find that you have a number of construction workers in your database and your company is coming out with heavy-duty hand cleaners, laundry detergent, and hand creams—it's only natural that you contact the customers in this group and let them know about this new product line.

Here is another example: Homemakers are the ones who purchase cleaning supplies, kitchen utensils, storage containers, decorating items, and products for children. Since homemakers live in single-income families, they might also be more interested in your less-expensive items.

Common Life Stages

You know which of your customers are young and which are old, but are you keeping track of what stage of life they are in and what is happening in their lives?

Newlyweds often live on fairly tight budgets, so messages about saving money are perfect for them. They might also like romantic items such as candles and incense. A line of practical items such as kitchen utensils or household tools might sell well to them, too. New parents and new empty-nesters have very distinct needs. So do new grandparents.

Also note that as people age they have different amounts of disposable income. People in their fifties and early sixties usually spend much more money on themselves and on gifts for their friends and family members than any other age group. Maybe it's time to sort through your database and send all these people a separate message.

Factors Unique to Your Product Line

Different product lines obviously lend themselves to different categories. For example, if you carry a line of health and beauty aids, you might want to split your customers by skin tone and hair type.

Or, if you carry cleaning supplies, you might note which of your customers are allergic to some items so that when your company comes out with hypoallergenic products you can communicate it immediately to the right customers.

What to Communicate to Which Customers

As you have probably guessed by now, there are an infinite number of ways to break up your customer database. The problem is that if you try to communicate a different message to every one of these categories, life will get too crazy.

You must make very judicious decisions. Sure, you discover that you have a dozen people who are all avid gardeners, and one of your products is a plant fertilizer. Great. But that product only provides you with 60 cents in commission for every sale and you have no other products that are specific to gardeners.

What do you do? Absolutely nothing. Oh, if you have space, you might mention the product in a mailing to customers, but it certainly isn't worth your time or money to go to any length to communicate this information to a group that will have such low payback for you.

FACTS

Choose the groups you will market based on the amount of money you will likely make if they buy. Products that bring you the most commission should always take precedence over other products, even if they are new and exciting.

Communicate Their Interest

Once you decide that a group has enough purchasing potential that they are worth a special message, it's time to decide what you will say to them. You want to communicate the fact that these people are somehow special by mentioning their specific "group" and the problems this group has that your products can solve. For example, if you're trying to sell laundry detergent to construction workers, start off by saying, "No one has a dirtier job than a construction worker. You love your work but you hate the grime on your clothes at the end of the day."

Next, tell them what you have and why you think it will meet their specific needs. "I have a laundry detergent that is specially formulated to clean heavy-duty grime."

ESSENTIALS

Keep your marketing message very short and to the point. You have grouped these people for one reason. Communicate only that reason and you will more likely make the sale.

You then need to tell your customers why this product is better than competing products: "And the best news is that it's almost half the price of the leading brand you can buy in the grocery store," or "And because it is made from all-natural ingredients, your clothes hold up longer and the detergent won't clog up your septic system."

Do not get carried away by listing a whole lot of items that they might be interested in. If they are new customers, you can include a catalog with their order. If they are old customers that you are trying to "bump up" into the next purchase group, they already know about your vast product line; they just need to know about this new development.

Think Creatively

Database marketing can be especially fun when you start to think creatively about your customers and what they might want. For example, you wouldn't communicate a sale on children's toys to people who are childless, but you might communicate it to every other group because they have children or possibly grandchildren. You might communicate it to everyone around the holidays because aunts and uncles need to provide gifts, too.

Likewise, you probably wouldn't routinely promote women's perfume to men, but it might be the right thing to do around Valentine's Day, Mother's Day, and Christmas.

Understanding Your Customers as They Change

Another reason you stay in touch with your customers and gather this information is that they will change. The customer who just became a grandfather is interested in many new items that you wouldn't have even tried selling to him when he was an empty-nester. The customer whose children become teenagers is interested in different items than when her children were toddlers.

Also look at your customers as they change careers or make other life changes. Did your customer's spouse just go back to work? That might signal a need for a whole new set of products. Did your customer just retire to a vacation home in Arizona? Again, a whole new set of products could be needed.

People change in ways that aren't always pleasant for them, but with sensitivity and an attitude of caring, the changes in their lives could bring you more business. Perhaps your "laggard" customer is under the weather. She suddenly might be very interested in buying more of your nutritional supplements. Likewise, a divorce turns one customer into two.

While you might be excited by the change in a customer's life because it means a chance to sell him more, try to be sensitive. Any change is stressful. As a result, avoid selling aggressively to people experiencing a life change—even if you believe that your products will help the customer deal with the change.

Means of Communication

Choose the means of communication according to your marketing message. Most often, it's best to send out postcards or short letters. E-mails also work well, especially if you are trying to sell just one item to a group of customers who all have e-mail addresses.

If the news is exciting and the group is small, you might choose to telephone each customer. Finally, you will note if a number of members of one of these groups is attending an upcoming sales party so you can tailor your presentation accordingly.

However, it's also important to stay in touch with your customers on a soft-sell basis. Many network marketers produce a simple one-page newsletter that includes information on new products and sales. You can then add a paragraph for each of the groups you want to separate out.

You also want to treat the customer as a friend even if you aren't exceptionally close. Stop in for a visit. Unlike the one-on-one sales call, this is simply a social visit. You might sell while you're there, but you are really there to catch up with the customer's life.

Send holiday cards; if you have your customers' birthday information, you can also send birthday cards with special offers on your products. If there is a major event such as a graduation or wedding, send a note of congratulations. Such messages will help you build a strong bond with your customer, ensuring continual customer loyalty and more potential sales in the future.

Good Customers Bring More Customers

Good customers are your best source of new leads. Look at your data closely and see if you can spot any signals that a specific customer would be good to pursue for new contacts. Is he a member of a social club that you haven't been in contact with? Does she have a vacation home in another community? Does his job bring him into contact with a group of people who aren't represented in your customer list yet?

The changes in your customers' lives are also opportunities for you to gain new prospects. Encourage someone starting a new job or moving to a new neighborhood to get to know coworkers and neighbors better by hosting a sales party. When someone celebrates a landmark birthday, suggest they hold a reunion of their high school friends along with a sales party. Some people actually prefer that to a traditional birthday party because your presentation provides something to talk about for people who may not have much in common anymore.

CHAPTER 18

It's All Down-Line from Here

No one ever became a millionaire through direct selling. If you want to make the serious money, you must work to regularly and consistently build an ever-larger down-line. As you scout for potential distributors to sponsor, choose your prospects carefully and treat them like gold—after all, they are your financial future!

Why Building a Down-Line Is Important

Your down-line is the key to your success in network marketing. Remember that you get a percentage of every person's sale when they are down the line from you. Consequently, you don't just want a lot of people in your down-line, you want a lot of good people who are capable of bringing in new recruits themselves.

Moreover, if you have worked hard on building your down-line, eventually you won't need to continue selling anymore. You will be working on motivating other people who are selling for you.

When it comes to a typical networking-marketing opportunity, you can recruit as many people as you want for your first line. These are the people you are sponsoring directly. Next to your personal commissions, you will typically receive the biggest commissions from their sales.

FACTS

You will never reach financial independence without a strong down-line. You can never sell enough products to make it worth your while to be a network marketer. Therefore, you must constantly recruit people to sell products so that you can earn money on their sales and on the sales of those they, in turn, sponsor.

The Pyramid Grows

The people recruited by your first line make up your second line, and you will receive a still-smaller commission from their sales. The structure continues, typically until about the seventh line, although some companies provide commissions as far as the twelfth line.

In addition, the commissions can change. Nearly every company offers the most commission from the first-line sales, but some will offer a slightly larger amount for the fourth line than for the third, for example. This is to encourage you to work with people farther down in your network and provide them with the wealth of experience you have gained during the time it's taken your network to get that large.

The First Attempt to Get a New Distributor

It's often easy for new distributors to sell the product. They start with their family and friends and build from there. However, when it comes time to sell the company program to a prospective new distributor, the challenge is more difficult and the whole process can be a little nerve-wracking.

QUESTIONS?

What if no one ever wants to be in my down-line?
It's common to fear that you will fail to recruit other distributors, but if you persist in your efforts, you will find those who are interested in joining. Remember, you need a little experience before anyone will see you as a good sponsor, so don't worry about finding other distributors for at least one year after you start.

Different organizations advocate different approaches to recruiting new distributors. Some, such as Amway, believe that you should surprise people with the benefits before you even tell them what the company is. Increasingly, however, the advice is that the decision to become a distributor should be based on facts and must be well thought out.

Chances are, you will have some indication that the person is interested in becoming a distributor. The person may have expressed interest during a sales party or during your one-on-one sales call. You might have followed up with everyone from a sales party by phone sometime the following week and found that one particular person was receptive to the idea.

Perhaps the person seems interested but says she isn't ready yet. In this case, you will want to keep in touch with her, offering incentives now and then to see if the time is right.

At each point, casually mention a benefit of becoming a distributor. When the person seems responsive, say you would love to talk to him more about it or even send him some information in the mail. Tell him that you just want to lay out the plans and talk about the benefits. You aren't looking for a commitment of any kind because you want him to be sure the opportunity is right for him.

Do not surprise the prospect with the presentation. While some network-marketing companies advocate telling the person you have "a great business idea" to tell them about, and no more, most people don't respond well to surprises.

Do Your Research

Treat this sale exactly as you would a product sale. Find out as much as you can about the person beforehand. If the person is a contact as a result of a sales party, call the host of the party and ask more questions about this person.

Also, don't hesitate to ask the prospects questions before you meet with them. Find out why they are interested in the opportunity, what sales experience they might have, where they live, what their family is like, and so on. Any information is good information because it can help you tailor the presentation.

Try to discover what would interest them most, then focus your presentation on those areas. In the beginning, some of the reasons people consider being a distributor are:

- Desire to be financially independent or to have extra spending money
- Desire to work for themselves
- Interest in the product
- A need to get out of the house and meet new people

Each of those reasons is very good but will certainly alter the presentation you give. For example, if you're talking to a housewife looking to get out of the house now and then and bring in a little extra spending money, your presentation on how to become a millionaire could just scare her off.

The Presentation

Again, some companies offer prepared presentations for their distributor prospects. However, these presentations can leave people cold because they tend to spend too much time on points the prospects don't care about and too little on those they do care about.

The best presentation is simply to sit across the table from the person, perhaps in a neutral setting such as a restaurant, and simply talk about the opportunities. Have all of the important areas outlined on a piece of paper. You should remember these because it wasn't that long ago that you were interested, too.

If you feel you need a backup, you can ask your sponsor to attend the meeting with you. However, some people see that as a high-pressure tactic, so be careful. If you pressure the person into becoming a distributor, she will likely drop out of the business very quickly. You want this to be a well-thought-out decision.

The Characteristics of a Good Recruit

Remember when you were trying to decide if network marketing was right for you? Now you will apply the same thoughts to the people you are looking to recruit. Look for people who have the following traits.

Perseverance

A good network marketer never gives up. He understands that there are good times and bad times in every business and that perseverance gets you through all of it.

When you are trying to determine if someone would be good for your down-line, look for someone who has shown perseverance in his or her life so far. You will know perseverance fairly quickly in a conversation with a potential recruit. He will exude determination. When you ask about this person's history, it will be colored with stories of difficult situations that the person has lived through and overcome.

Of course, not everyone has had a chance to show perseverance in some dramatic fashion. Some people have had relatively easy lives, especially if they are still fairly young. In order to judge if these people have perseverance, try to find out more about their upbringing and their parents.

It's not difficult to recognize people who lack perseverance. They are the ones who quit piano lessons because they were too hard, drop out of karate because it got too difficult, and quit every job they had the second things got rough. They probably got divorced without even trying to make the marriage work. In short, if they are quitters in other areas of life, they likely will be quitters as a network marketers, too.

FACTS

Perseverance is the most important trait in a network marketer. You must have recruits who are willing to work through their problems and will keep going when times get tough. If someone always gives up easily, he is very likely to quit network marketing in the near future.

Passion and Enthusiasm

Network marketing takes a great deal of enthusiasm because you often have to overcome people's disinterest and natural objections to buying from a "door-to-door salesperson."

Enthusiasm is another trait that is very easy to identify in people. Just ask them about their family and their hobbies. If their voices rise, they start smiling as they talk, and they get very excited, you know they have passion.

People who lack passion and enthusiasm will probably not succeed in network marketing. They may want a change of job and think that they might like working for themselves, but they aren't really excited about the prospect and in a few months you'll hear them complaining about network marketing in the same way they complained about their no-future corporate jobs.

Outgoing Nature

There's no question about it. If you want to succeed in network marketing, you have to be able to get out there and meet people. If the person likes being a loner, they probably wouldn't like network marketing.

While exceptionally outgoing people are often the centers of attention at parties, many people are outgoing even though they don't like parties. Some people prefer to socialize in small groups. Others are drawn out of their shells once someone draws them into conversation.

The difference between an outgoing person and a recluse is whether they enjoy people. Outgoing people are interested in others. They ask lots of questions, show interest in what you have to say, and like to learn new things.

Instead of looking for party animals, look for people who get out and do things. If they have taken a community education class, joined a club, or volunteered at a nursing home recently, it would be safe to assume that these are outgoing people. They aren't afraid of being in a situation where they don't know anyone.

SSENTIALS If someone doesn't like meeting new people, they probably won't like network marketing. The ideal network marketer finds everyone they meet fascinating. Encourage people who like to work alone to look into other self-employment options.

Listening Skills

Whether they are selling a product, selling the company to a prospective recruit, or helping one of their own "down-liners" make it through a difficult time, a network marketer must know how to listen. This means paying attention, trying to figure out what the problem is, knowing what clues signal a true need, and being able to read between the lines and interpret body language.

True listeners will know what you are trying to say even when you aren't saying a word. As you tell an emotional story, they will be able to relate to what happened. They will add insightful thoughts about how you must have felt or how they would have felt in a similar circumstance.

A good listener also instinctively does things like remember your name and what you do for a living. He or she will remember little details you have let slip, such as the ages of your children or where you went to college.

On the other hand, someone who doesn't listen usually dominates the conversation as its only topic. Such a person will probably forget your name soon after you've introduced yourself and may even repeat a question he or she asked a few minutes earlier.

Creativity

When it comes to prospecting for new members of your down-line or trying to break into a new community with your product, it takes creativity to figure out what will work. Ideally, you want someone in your down-line who can build on your own creativity, add ideas, and create a synergy with you and others in your down-line so that, in the end, your network is greater than the sum of its parts.

You can recognize creative people in many ways. One obvious clue is their hobbies. Do they read mysteries, poetry, or science fiction? Do they do creative things, such as play a musical instrument, sew their own clothes, or do oil painting?

FACTS

People who aren't creative can be valuable assets as long as they have many of the other needed traits. However, don't expect them to think outside the box when you're developing new sales strategies.

Another clue is the way the person dresses. Creative people usually love color and will have a splash of color in their wardrobe at even the most formal event. Truly creative people stand out in a crowd; they often wear bright colors or interesting jewelry and accessories.

While creative people love to break little, inconsequential rules (like jumping in the swimming pool after hours), uncreative people live and die by the rules. That can be a problem, because there are few rules in network marketing. These people would constantly be asking you how something has to be done when you actually want them to come up with their own good ideas.

Communication Skills

Business is all about communication—and this is especially true in network marketing. You want someone who knows how to communicate a message to prospects. You want someone who will communicate with you when he has a problem. And you want someone who will communicate with her own down-line so that they become big producers, too.

Ask some leading questions to discover whether a prospective distributor is a good communicator. For example, find out about his last job. How did he communicate with his peers and his boss? Also ask about his family. How does he communicate with his children and his spouse?

You don't want someone who tries to ignore problems or who believes in "survival of the fittest." You want people who are very willing to admit they need help and who believe that people make better decisions with more information.

Willingness to Learn

No matter how well versed the potential recruit is in business strategies and sales techniques, she probably knows just a small fraction of what is necessary to become a success in network marketing.

Consequently, you need to look for someone who likes to learn new things. To discover if this is the case, simply ask them what the last new thing was that they learned. A lifetime learner will immediately start to list everything from taking violin and tango lessons to reading about new theories in supercomputing.

At the same time, a lifetime learner will quickly tell you that she loves to learn and can't imagine not constantly working to learn something new. These people take classes, lessons, and seminars just for fun.

You want to steer clear of people who don't like to learn, because they will be far more work than they are worth to you. You will have to fight them at every step to get them to learn new sales strategies and even to learn new product information.

Ability to Live the Job

Most people like to work set hours and spend the rest of the time doing what they want. Network marketers, however, are always open to opportunities. They work odd hours and can switch into work mode the second someone asks about what products they sell. They may be at a cousin's wedding, making idle chitchat, but the second someone shows interest in their work, the wedding guest becomes a salesperson.

A good way to tell if a person can live the job is to look at her current job. Does she talk about it at home? Does she work on problems after hours? If the person has a job with set hours, does he like to putter around with his hobby during odd hours?

You might actually ask the person how he feels about working "twenty-four/seven." It's important to have balance in your home and work life, of course, but if the person is absolutely unwilling to work odd hours, this might not be the job for him.

Ability to Put Worry Aside

During the first few years, network marketing is unpredictable, especially in terms of money. If the person tends to worry about little things, he probably wouldn't like network marketing. After all, network marketers have very little control over what their down-line does, and they can't force people to buy from them.

You'll recognize a worrier immediately, because she will worry about the cleanliness of the restaurant you're meeting at, whether it's going to rain on the weekend, or how she will pay for junior's college. Chances are, worriers won't even consider network marketing beyond the initial examination, because the thought of unpredictable cash flow will scare them away.

Flexibility

In the lives of network marketers, no two days are ever the same. Your recruit must be able to move from one thing to the next in a split second. That's why housewives often make such good recruits—they are used to balancing many tasks and changing their priorities in a split second.

Look for someone who always seems to have a lot of irons in the fire. It doesn't matter what those irons are—children, pets, hobbies, friends, jobs, or something else. What matters is that the person knows how to balance many things at once and enjoys the constant change.

Making the Sale

Selling new recruits is exactly like selling your product, only a little more difficult because you are asking people to do more than spend a few dollars. You are asking them to make a life change. As a result, you will want to look for people who are in need of a change. Signs that a person needs a change include the following:

- They say they are burned out.
- They are new to town.
- They are newly retired.
- They have teenagers.
- They are newly diagnosed with a chronic disease.
- They have been in the same job for ten or more years.

This is just the first cut. These people might be looking for something new. But then again, they might be perfectly happy, so you don't want to rush into a sales presentation just yet.

Judging Interest

If you're lucky, the person is already a customer of yours and knows how wonderful the product is. Or, this person is already looking for the right network-marketing opportunity and has approached you at a conference or even at your son's soccer game. Or, if you are a little less lucky, your prospect may be a sales-party guest who is only mildly interested. In all of these cases, you know what the prospect's interests are.

Don't pressure people who show no interest in becoming a distributor after you have approached them with the idea. It would probably take too much of your precious time to convince them. Simply wait a year or two and try again.

From time to time, you will also meet people who you know would make perfect distributors. Whether it's a man you meet at your nephew's baptism or a woman your friend points out to you at a recent sales party, these people fit every criterion for a good distributor. And yet, they don't show the slightest interest when you casually mention to them the opportunities of network marketing.

If they did show interest in the products you sell and are obviously in need of change in their career, just be straightforward and tell them that you think they would make a great distributor. They likely will let you know right away if they are even a tiny bit interested. If the idea is totally abhorrent to them, they will let you know that, too. Then you can politely change the subject and possibly sell them some product anyway.

Examining Their Personality

If the person seems interested in becoming a distributor, you next need to determine how you will actually sell him on the opportunity. Let's review the basic personality types from Chapter 15—helpers, prima donnas, trendsetters, and contemplators. Just as in a sales situation, the personality of the prospective distributor is directly associated with what in particular will make network marketing an enticing opportunity.

Helpers will be looking for a way to help others. You might talk about how the product is high quality and offers people a chance to actually save money, how they can help young mothers who are on a budget feed their families, or how they can help the elderly stay healthy longer.

FACTS

People have different reasons for becoming network marketers. Usually they are looking for a change that will let them lead a life that is more appropriate for their personality type. If you can sell this opportunity to their personality, you have a good chance of gaining a new recruit.

Prima donnas want to be popular and noticed. Talk up the social aspects of being a distributor as well as the money potential. Talk about the "big cheeses" who go to all the international conventions, who have had their photos on the cover of magazines such as *Entrepreneur*, and who win all those glamorous trips. Talk about how a distributor can build a large down-line and may have hundreds or even thousands of people working "for" him or her.

Trendsetters want to be the first on the block to have something. Bring out the magazine articles and materials that talk about the differences between your product line and competing products. If your company is older and well established, talk about all the research the company does to constantly come up with new items. Also talk about the fact that network marketing is one of the biggest business trends for the twenty-first century.

Contemplators want all the facts and comparison data before they buy. Consequently, you need to lay it all out for them, including the compensation plan and any product research data. Give them everything you have. Offer to get them more stuff from the home office. Check on the Web, at the library, and anywhere else to see if there is more information about your company, your products, or even the product category's growth potential. Give them this book and encourage them to analyze the company.

Dealing with Second Thoughts

Your recruits will likely have second thoughts. You probably had second thoughts yourself, so why shouldn't they?

In such a situation, what they need is encouragement. "I believe in you" and "You can do it" are wonderful little phrases that can make the difference between a maybe and a yes.

Remember that people don't have to start out being as enthusiastic as you were. Perhaps your newest recruit wants to just give it a try. That's okay as long as you remind her that the only way to financial freedom is through steady progress.

Don't pressure a person who is having second thoughts about becoming a distributor. Answer her questions and try to encourage her, but if you pressure a potential recruit at this point, you may scare her away for good.

If someone is having serious second thoughts, it's best to say, "I think you should think about it a little while longer." By giving him a chance to relax, you might just help him to make the decision more quickly.

Training the Recruit

Your network-marketing company likely offers a packet of information that serves as product training as well as basic information on how to fill out order forms and the like. It is absolutely essential that the new recruit goes over this information several times. You might want to spend an afternoon going through the information with the person to make sure she has it all down and has no questions.

It's also likely that your company offers some sort of sales training. Encourage the new recruit to take advantage of any sales training that is available. Even if he has sold in other settings, there is always something new that can be learned, especially when the training is tailored directly to the product the new distributor will be selling.

If sales training isn't available through the company, find a program offered by your local chamber of commerce or a local business association. Virtually every medium- and large-sized town in the nation has several sales-training events offered every year that are specifically designed for new salespeople.

You and Your Shadow

In the meantime, as the new recruit is getting up to speed on the product information, you can show her what good sales skills are by having her shadow you for a few days. Introduce her as a new distributor when you make a presentation, then have her watch exactly what you do. After the presentation, ask her to critique what you did and let her ask you any questions about why you approached something the way you did.

QUESTIONS?

How can I give good training if I'm still new to it myself?
Turn to your own sponsor and others in your up-line to get ideas you can pass on to your down-line. Also, hold brainstorming sessions with your down-line members so you can learn from each other.

Also, invite your new recruit to spend a few hours with you in the office. Show her your workspace, how you put together a presentation, how you analyze the people at a sales party, and how you do some basic prospecting.

Ongoing Training

As your recruit becomes more and more comfortable with the job, it's time to start adding more sophisticated training. Here are a few suggestions:

- Keep your eyes open for other national sales and marketing training seminars that go beyond basic selling skills.
- Produce a newsletter for your down-line that contains information you have gleaned from sales and marketing magazines, seminars, and talk shows. Include tips you have discovered for overcoming objections and invite others in your down-line to contribute to the newsletter, too.
- Hold monthly seminars for your down-line members where you discuss new products and sales challenges. Invite the attendees to train each other on various techniques they have learned.

Motivation Techniques

Many people are unclear about what motivation is and how it works. They tend to think that we are all motivated by money. In fact, most people are motivated by what money can buy, and even then it's typically not the object that is purchased but the emotions that go with it. For example, a big house or an expensive car brings prestige. Financial independence brings more family time, which, in turn, brings more love and bonding.

Consequently, motivation to simply make money doesn't really work. As you motivate a particular individual, you need to understand the underlying reason for why he or she wants that money and then continue to promote that.

Personality Differences

That reason is tied into each person's personality type. If you know what sold a person on becoming a distributor, you know what to do to keep him motivated now. Just reinforce those same ideas again and again.

Helpers want to know they are doing good for someone or for the world; when helpers get discouraged, you need to tell them how much you appreciate their hard work and remind them how much the products they sell are helping people.

Prima donnas want to know they are making a big splash in the world; when they get discouraged, ask them to make a presentation at your next monthly meeting to discuss how they overcame price objections.

Trendsetters want to know they are pursuing (and acquiring) the latest and greatest; when trendsetters get discouraged, remind them about the purchases they just made with the money from this job.

Contemplators want to know that when everything is tallied up, they are doing better than average; when contemplators get discouraged, tell them they are doing better than any recruit you've ever had.

Other Motivators

Everyone is motivated by praise, at least to some extent—that's why so many sales programs have awards attached to them. You can do the same thing with your own down-line group by giving an award at every meeting.

Meetings are another form of motivation. People like to socialize with others who are like them. The meetings are a chance to learn, but they are also a chance to feel like part of a group and to feel like a professional.

Perhaps the most important motivator, though, is simply staying in touch with your down-line. Let them know that you care about their success and that you aren't just expecting them to work hard so you can make more money.

CHAPTER 19

Be a Survivor

Ever wonder why so many people are *former* network marketers? It's because they gave up. Maybe they didn't reach their goals because they didn't work smartly and efficiently. Or maybe they allowed a few slow periods to get them down. Whatever the case, don't let it happen to you. Keep your nose to the grindstone and remember that you'd rather be one of the success stories than one of the quitters.

Why People Give Up

People give up for many reasons—because they aren't meeting their goals, because they don't have any goals and no vision, or because the process is slow and requires a lot of hard work, more than they expected.

But if everyone gave up the second a job got hard or took too long, then no one would ever be a success. Remember, there are no miracles in this business. Network marketing is work—it is unpredictable and requires effort.

Of course, there are good reasons for giving up. Perhaps you have just won the lottery. Well, network marketing is fun, but you certainly don't need to work at it too hard now! Other good reasons are a serious illness or landing the corporate job of your dreams.

QUESTIONS?

What if I discover I really hate this work?
Before you give up, try to figure out what aspects of network marketing you dislike and see if another family member or a friend might team up with you to do that work. If you like prospecting and your spouse likes sales, together you'll make a great team.

The important thing to remember is that network marketing is always there for you. If it isn't working for you at the moment, you can always take a break and go back to it when you feel that you are ready.

The Bad Sponsor

Sometimes there are serious obstacles on your way to being successful in this field. For instance, it may be that you want to quit because of your sponsor. Unscrupulous sponsors sometimes mislead prospective distributors in order to build up their down-line. They promise the novices lots of easy money, building them up for disappointment and failure.

In another scenario, a sponsor may be a decent person who has prepared you for what's to come, but thinks that getting you started in network marketing is all that needs to be done. When you try to reach such a sponsor, you'll never get a response. These sponsors simply don't see the value of motivating you. Many can be turned around if you simply remind them that when you sell more, they make more money. It's to their advantage to help keep you motivated.

Having a bad sponsor does not mean that you have to give up this network-marketing opportunity. It just means you will have to look elsewhere for guidance and motivation. You might find it farther "up the line," or you might have to develop the motivation within yourself.

Worries and Stress

Some people give up because they finally realize the magnitude of their decision to get involved in network marketing—that their life is undergoing a deep change—and they panic. Say you have given up a full-time job with good benefits and a nice retirement package and now you find yourself sitting in your spare bedroom wondering how you will make those mortgage payments.

FACTS

Time heals all wounds. If you keep working, you will succeed. You will work through this difficult time and find yourself looking back and wondering what you were so concerned about.

If you were realistic before you went into this opportunity, you will be prepared financially for the slow periods when cash flow is low and your spirits are no higher. Everyone has a bit of a letdown when the excitement of the new opportunity wears off. You probably felt the same thing when you started your last "real" job, too.

If you do fall into a period of panic and self-doubt, simply revisit the original reasons you had for taking this opportunity. Look at your goals. Revisit your affirmations. Make a list of all the wonderful things happening in your life now, such as meeting new people, having more time for family, and having control over your future.

The Job That Dwindles

Some people don't quit network marketing, it just sort of wanders out of their lives. These are the people who weren't really committed to begin with. They thought they could sell a little bit on the side to make some extra money, and they didn't realize that they were taking on a new job, with all the responsibilities that such an endeavor involves.

If you find yourself spending less and less time with the job, you are falling into the most common failure trap among network marketers. The job dwindles because you lose momentum, not because it was wrong for you. Reassess your situation to see if you truly want to become financially independent—perhaps that was never your serious objective.

**SSENTIALS**

> You won't quit this opportunity if you made the right decision to begin with. If you truly have the personality that is right for network marketing, you won't let the initial panic attack and the downtimes force you out of the opportunity.

Even if that's the case, don't feel too bad. This may not have been the right time for you to get into network marketing. That doesn't mean it's wrong for you, though. It just means that you need to reassess what you really want from this opportunity and set new goals.

A change in your life's circumstances might force you to give up network marketing for a while. However, before giving it up completely, consider scaling down your hours so you can keep your hand in it in case you want to come back to it as a full-time occupation.

When the Company Quits

Perhaps the saddest situations are when the network-marketing company goes out of business and you lose your products and with them your down-line and your job. Not only do you have the same feelings of betrayal that you might have had when you were laid off from a corporate job, but there is no severance package to help you through these times.

If you have done your research well, chances are, this won't happen to you. However, things do go wrong in even the most successful of companies. Sometimes it is as simple as a change in the marketplace that the company wasn't prepared to handle. Suddenly its product isn't of value to many people and the company is forced out of the market.

No matter how great your company and how long it has been in the market, you need to be prepared for the worst. If this happens to you, try not to give up on network marketing. Just do a more thorough job of researching your next opportunity. You already know that you like the work and can do it well—losing a company is definitely a setback, but it's not the end of the world.

How to Stay Motivated

You can't be motivated every day of your life. However, you *can* carry with you an overall sense of motivation that you will succeed at network marketing in the long-term.

Always remember your vision statement. Carry a copy of it with you everywhere you go. If you're discouraged because your last commission check was for $3.72, pull out your vision statement and refocus.

FACTS

No one is motivated all the time. If they seem as if they are, it's because they are very good at faking it. Sometimes you just need to smile and do the job. Suddenly you will find that the job is getting done and you really feel like smiling.

Working Through Tough Times

The biggest cure for these discouraging times is to work. Even if you aren't getting a lot of sales, you can keep yourself busy with the business by ferreting out good prospects, developing marketing materials, and trying to improve your sales presentations.

Don't give yourself time to worry. Just look ahead and work toward the goals you first set. Do something for the business every day, even if is extremely difficult to sit down at the computer or pick up the phone. Once you get started, you'll be surprised how easy it is to keep going.

When things aren't going well, the temptation is to assume nothing will go well. However, bad times usually pass—although not as quickly as we'd like—but you need to work through them. Instead of giving up, make a resolution that you will keep working.

Sure, the work is harder than you expected and you are getting discouraged because all you seem to do is work hard—harder than you did at your "real" job—and you aren't seeing big financial gains yet. Remember that you are setting a stage for future growth. It could take years to build this foundation, but once it's built, life will be much easier.

Try New Marketing Tactics

If your business is in a slump, instead of looking for a new occupation, find a new opportunity within the business. For example, try a new marketing strategy (as described in Chapter 17). One Mary Kay salesperson, for example, started calling on the parents of young girls who took dance lessons. The girls all needed makeup for their recitals and the parents wanted a high-quality product for their little girls' faces.

**SSENTIALS** Try a new sales tactic, too. Maybe you have been relying on sales parties but the summer has arrived and people are too busy to get together for sales events. Try setting up booths at local county fairs or community events. If you have a vacation home, grab your catalog and go visit your vacation-home neighbors.

Working with Your Sponsor

Your sponsor should be your chief motivator. He is the person you can call when you want to quit, when you're in tears, or when you wonder why you ever got into this to begin with.

Your sponsor should be a font of wisdom, because she has been in the business longer than you. Ask how she handled the downtime. How did he crash through barriers? What advice does she have for giving you a boost?

It's also your sponsor's job to make you feel good about yourself. Even if she doesn't have any secrets for jump-starting your business, she should at least meet you for lunch and listen to your concerns while reminding you that you are a very capable person who has a lot going for you.

In short, your sponsor should be your champion. He should tell you how smart you are, how good you're doing, how proud he is of you, and how it would be a complete disaster if you left network marketing because you are the perfect person to succeed at this opportunity.

More Substantial Assistance

You can also ask your sponsor to work with you to overcome your current slump. Here are a few ideas:

- *Have your sponsor make a sales call with you.* Afterwards, ask him how he thinks you did and what you could improve upon.
- *Ask for a leg up.* Perhaps the sponsor has a hot prospect she can send your way. Or maybe there's an upcoming event such as a county fair that the sponsor would "share" with you.
- *Look at your sponsor's database for ideas.* How does the sponsor categorize his customers? Does it give you any ideas?
- *Ask the sponsor to host a party.* Why not? Just because she sells the products too, it doesn't mean she can't invite friends over to buy from you.
- *Ask your sponsor to attend sales training with you.* Often, when two or more people from the same company attend a training event, the trainer concentrates on their needs more than individuals in the group, so you get more good advice for the money.

Look for Additional Help

Your sponsor is not the only person who can help you deal with a bad spell. Even if you are single and have just moved to a new town, there are many people you can turn to for help to get through a slack period in your business.

As with every other aspect of your work, you must take action if you are going to get through this time. Sit down and make a list of people you can turn to for moral support as well as advice; then pick up the phone and make the call.

You will be surprised at how much people like to help. Very few people will kick you when you're down. Even complete strangers will offer advice and will boost your self-esteem if you need it. All you have to do is ask.

Family and Friends

If your family and friends support your new endeavor, they will be there for you when times are tough. Be honest and tell them that things are slower than you had hoped. Ask what they have done in their lives when they have been in similar situations. Do they have a favorite quote or book that helped them get through a discouraging time?

And don't forget that your friends have friends. Perhaps you have a friend who knows a successful salesperson. You could arrange lunch with that friend of a friend just to get a little moral support or maybe even get some insights on how to better sell your products.

Also remember to visit your elders. It can sound corny, but there is nothing like hearing about all the problems your grandfather had—when he lost his business in the recession in the 1970s, got fired from his job at fifty-five, and had to work until he was well into his seventies because he had no retirement plan. If your grandfather survived all that, you can certainly survive your ordeal.

Steer clear of family and "friends" who are likely to say "I told you so." Unfortunately we all seem to have a few people in our lives who enjoy watching us fail, so avoid them until your business has taken off.

Your Customers

Yes, your customers can be a source of motivation. Contact some of your best customers and talk about the product line. Encourage your best customer to have a sales party. Give yourself a chance to get enthusiastic about the opportunity again.

Chances are, you have made some good friends among your best customers. Set a date to introduce them to a new product but plan to spend much of the time talking about life. Tell them you're a bit discouraged. Ask what they have done when they hit a slow period in their lives.

FACTS

Customers are a wonderful source of motivation. You can see and hear firsthand how your product and your presence has changed their lives. If you're feeling discouraged, host your own sales party and gather your best customers!

Your customers will remind you why you got into this business to begin with. They will thank you for introducing them to such a great product. They will tell you how much they look forward to getting your brochures and catalogs. They will tell you that you can't quit because then they'd have to find someone else who sells the same product.

Your Down-Line

One woman was getting very down on herself because she hadn't been meeting her sales goals for the last few months. One of her down-line distributors called her and started talking about how exciting it was that for the first time in her life she had extra spending money. She was going to get a manicure. She felt so wonderful.

Suddenly the woman realized that meeting her sales goals wasn't her one and only reason for working in network marketing. She truly enjoyed the fact that she was helping other women lead happy, productive lives.

Look at your down-line and see if you have inspired anyone to make good changes in his or her life. Did an abused housewife gain the self-esteem to leave her husband once she started making money for herself? Was one of your down-line members able to send his son to college with no loans as a result of the business? Did another build the house of her dreams? Have members of your down-line taken vacations or purchased luxury items they always wanted because you introduced them to this opportunity?

Other Sales Professionals

Sales can be a lonely, misunderstood profession, and most towns have an organization of professional salespeople who meet periodically as a social group that offers its members emotional support.

These people are wonderful company who will make you realize that you are not alone in your discouragement. They also can tell you what has helped them make it through tough times.

SSENTIALS

Misery loves company. Search out other businesspeople who can relate to your situation. Drown your sorrows together. Talk about your problems. You may not feel better, but you will at least know that you aren't alone.

In addition, these groups bring in speakers to talk about motivation because that is the single biggest problem salespeople share. They also will recommend Web sites and books that can help you through difficult times.

Business and Social Groups

Are you a member of the Rotary Club, the Jaycees, or the Knights of Columbus? If you're feeling down about your work, resist the temptation to stay home. You have no reason to be embarrassed by the situation. In fact, if you confide in some people during the meeting that you're feeling depressed about your job, you may get some good advice.

Even if you decide not to talk about your job situation, you might feel better just by getting out and being with other people. You will remember that there is more to life than money and work.

Peers in the Business

You have probably met other members of your sponsor's down-line at a meeting or another event. These are the people who truly know what you are going through. They will not only understand that you're discouraged because business is slow, they will understand what that means to your family and everyone else in your life. Ask for any ideas they have that helped jump-start their business when things were slow; also find out how they managed to get through a "funk" without damaging their relationships with others.

Business Experts

The world is jam-packed with business experts, especially when it comes to sales and motivation. Attend a seminar. Visit a Web site. Read a book. You can turn to some of the time-proven classics such as Dale Carnegie's *How to Win Friends and Influence People* or Larry Wilson's *The One Minute Salesperson.*

Also, don't forget to sign up for some good training. Both Dale Carnegie Training and Wilson Learning offer excellent sales courses that are good for network marketers. Many other consultants and training organizations offer training that fits the needs of people in direct sales. (See Appendix A for additional resources.)

FACTS

Just because they aren't in your same field of business doesn't mean they don't have good ideas for staying motivated and direct selling. Look for the gems in every business book and magazine article you read. If you find just one thing to emulate, that's a success.

Read business magazines for inspiration. *Entrepreneur,* for example, often features success stories of network marketers. Read some of these profiles to see if you can find something that would work in your business.

Re-evaluate Your Goals

Don't hesitate to reset your goals. Sometimes we are so excited when we start a new opportunity that we set very ambitious sales goals. And that's fine—it's not at all a bad way to start. However, things can change. If this is a part-time business for you, you might discover that you don't have the time to meet those goals. There's no harm in backing off a little if you have to.

Don't feel as though you have to stay with the goals you initially set for the business. If you truly can't reach them, reset them to a more reasonable level, but don't get discouraged and give them up.

Personal or world events may sometimes demand a goal change. Perhaps you are recovering from a serious illness. By all means, don't be discouraged that you didn't meet last month's goals.

Business issues can be good reasons for changing your goals. You thought your product was unique, but a major manufacturer has just released the identical product at a lower price. There are ways to combat that, but it could very likely cut into your financial goals for at least a few months.

Don't be concerned if you find yourself resetting your goals often, especially in the first year or so of being in business. We all need to step back and reassess our lives periodically, so this is a natural process.

CHAPTER 20

The Future of Network Marketing

Network marketing is a force of the future. As more people look to work for themselves and more companies look for unique ways to market their products, network marketing will become a natural move for many people. At the same time, the Internet and other mass-marketing tactics will make network marketing easier than ever before.

Traditional No More

It's rare that a company will move from retail sales to network marketing. However, a few have done just that when they found themselves competing against well-entrenched corporate giants.

When both MCI and Sprint decided to compete with AT&T for long-distance phone services, they chose a network-marketing approach. Management determined that it was the quickest way to compete with the telecommunications giant because people would only change their loyalty to AT&T if they were even more loyal to the person selling them.

Citigroup had similar reasons when it used network marketing to sell its credit card services. Instead of traditional blind mail and Internet offers, it used the face-to-face aspect of network marketing to build sales faster. Interestingly, some people were willing to take a slightly higher interest rate in exchange for knowing the person who sold them the credit card.

FACTS

Traditional companies are beginning to look at network marketing as a viable option for quickly expanding sales in a confusing, fast-changing marketplace. Network marketing prevents problems that companies face when expanding into global marketplaces and adjusts to consumer needs more quickly than other sales strategies.

Likewise, when a plastics manufacturer decided to expand its sales into some international markets, it turned to network marketing. One reason is that network marketers provide access to people that retail outlets can't. In addition, they are much better at building customer relationships and are able to convince people to buy something they have never tried before much faster than salespeople who rely on other marketing strategies.

In the Business Marketplace

Today, network marketing is a multibillion-dollar business. A global computer search of multilevel marketing companies just a few years ago yielded about 1,000 names. Today, the number is closer to 10,000.

The reason for this rapid growth is simple: Network marketing serves not only to bring products to consumers who otherwise wouldn't have access to them, but also provides companies with a method of distribution unparalleled in the more traditional marketplace. Instead of looking to set up large corporate divisions in far-flung locations, network marketing naturally grows the company for the business.

Network marketing also provides a time-proven strategy for entering new markets with a wide range of existing products as well as brand-new items. If a company decides to expand its product line, there are no issues of retraining salespeople or adding distributors. That is already done for the company through the network-marketing strategy.

ESSENTIALS

Network marketing helps a company learn a marketplace and test it out before going in with traditional marketing tactics. In many cases, companies find that it is the only strategy to reach large groups of consumers who aren't accustomed to shopping in large stores.

Network marketing also brings a high degree of adaptability. There is no fear of entering a new marketplace, because it isn't new to the people doing the selling. Consequently, companies don't have to worry that their sales literature is about benefits that a specific culture doesn't care about or that their sales tactics will somehow offend a specific religious group. The salesperson is already a part of that group and, because she is self-employed, would simply choose not to use a strategy that would offend her friends.

The Global Advantage

Network marketing provides an easy method for a company to enter the global marketplace. Not only does it naturally avoid a cultural faux pas (do you remember how Chevrolet tried to sell the Nova—which translates as "doesn't run" in Spanish—in Mexico?), but it provides a means of distribution in countries that traditional companies may not understand.

For example, how does a company whose products are carried only through large retail chains such as Wal-Mart and Target expect to sell its products in Russia, India, and China? All three of these countries provide excellent opportunities and growing customer bases, but they also have large populations that live in rural areas with no large discount-store chains.

The answer, of course, is network marketing. All it takes is one person in a geographic area to sell to others, no matter how far they are from a major city. If it's a product people truly value, they will wait the days or even weeks for it to be delivered.

It's Cost-Efficient

Network marketing costs very little for a company to implement. All that is necessary is the basic marketing materials for the salespeople to use. Beyond that, there are no real expenses for the company. Every commission check to a salesperson is covered by the fact that the product was actually sold; it isn't sitting in some retail store waiting to be returned at the end of the season.

ESSENTIALS

Because costs are relatively low, many companies may decide to compete against corporate giants when they otherwise would have walked away from the market. Furthermore, network marketing allows companies to offer more products than they would through a traditional sales strategy.

Introducing new products requires minimal additional costs necessary for updated marketing materials and perhaps the sales training, but that is nothing compared to the costs traditional companies face when they are introducing a new item to the market.

Finally, there are no distribution costs for the company. Yes, the company pays to ship the product to the salesperson or even to the customer, but the customer pays those costs up front.

It's Technology-Friendly

Network marketing is a natural option for today's technology-oriented environment. Computers, telephones, faxes, personal digital assistants, digital cameras, and virtually every other piece of technology that makes our lives easier provides an advantage in network marketing.

Thanks to technology, network marketers have the means to reach thousands of people in very little time. There is no more door-to-door selling. Now people can read a sales pitch by logging onto their computer, answering their voice mail, or checking their fax machines.

In short, there is no reason not to use network marketing. In the past, a company may have felt network marketing produced slower sales than retail outlets because it required a one-on-one interaction between the distributor and the customer, but that just isn't the case anymore. Today's high-tech network marketer can reach more people in an hour than a retail store on a good day.

It Works for Internet-Based Companies

With network-marketing techniques, Internet-based companies are quickly able to jump the most difficult hurdle in the industry—getting people to visit their Web sites. Amazon.com and PayPal.com were the first to realize that network marketing is the best strategy for getting their names and services known to as many people as possible in a very short time.

FACTS

Network marketing saw a big boost with the rise of Internet-based companies. Many found that it was the quickest, most cost-effective way to get their names out there and to ensure that people would actually visit their sites.

In the case of PayPal.com, for example, the company offered $5 for every person who mentioned your name when he or she signed up for an account. Note that signing up costs nothing and is no guarantee that you would ever use the account, so there was no reason not to let your sister, best friend, or neighbor get her $5 that could be used for any number of online stores.

It's Entrepreneur-Friendly

In today's corporate-driven world, it's not easy to break into the marketplace with a new product. The ranks of entrepreneurs are rife with people who truly had made better mousetraps but found themselves stomped into oblivion by multimillion-dollar marketing campaigns. Others found that their corporate competitors could easily sap an entrepreneur's budget by filing frivolous "noncompete" lawsuits.

However, network marketing can quickly and easily spread a product around the world, because there are no extra liabilities for the entrepreneur. If the item is truly good and people want it, the network will build quickly and all that the entrepreneur has to worry about is producing enough products to keep up with demand.

This is especially advantageous in today's world because technology is allowing so many new products to be developed so quickly. Engineers who in the past would have needed millions of dollars in equipment can now set off on their own and develop products with just a few thousand dollars.

A Better Form of Employment

It's no longer a secret that many corporations and business executives don't really have the best interests of their employees at heart. Because of that, people are looking for ways to control their own destinies outside of the corporate world. Many don't even want to become millionaires; they just want to make a nice income on their own terms, with no fear of layoffs, unemployment, and vanishing pensions.

People are also looking for ways to get more out of life. They want to create a balance of work and personal time. They want to reap the rewards of life and all that it has to offer.

When Hard Work Is Rewarded

People also want to be rewarded for the work they do. And yet, most employees know that no matter how hard they work, their salary likely won't reflect their toils. The best they can hope for is a raise that is a few percentage points higher than the annual inflation.

Business magazines are filled with stories of people who are paid by the hour and are expected to take their work home, to complete it on their own time, because corporate executives are trying to get those bonuses for spending less company money. These same hourly workers see their production quotas rising as their work teams are slimmed down.

As more people become concerned about the ethics of large corporations, they will likely turn to small-business opportunities that provide them with the chance to set their own rules. As a result, look for even more network-marketing opportunities in the near future.

Salaried employees know that if they work harder, the most they will see for it is a raise and maybe a bonus at the end of the year, but there are no immediate rewards for missing their daughter's dance recital or their son's soccer game.

Even professional salespeople are being asked to work harder for their money. Quotas are set higher than ever and commissions are low. Bonuses are tiny or nearly impossible to obtain as companies try to get more work out of fewer employees.

Network Marketing Meets Social Needs

People are also tired of working in an impersonal environment of cubicles and computer networks. We are all social creatures. We want to have personal connections in our working lives just as much as in our personal lives.

Network marketing allows distributors to do just that. While selling products, distributors are also creating bonds with their customers and among themselves (after all, each distributor has a down-line and an up-line of other network marketers). Network marketing provides an opportunity to reach out and offer advice and practical solutions—and even companionship—in a large, impersonal world as well as providing a network of people you can call upon whenever you need it.

Network Marketing Meets Family Values

The same is true with our families. As people are asked to work more and more hours for the same—or less—money, families are suffering. Children don't connect with their parents and siblings as they spend more and more time at day care centers or doing organized activities designed to keep the kids busy while their parents are at work.

Network marketing, however, lets a family be a family again. You can run your business on your own schedule, making time for soccer games and dance recitals. If junior gets into trouble at school, you can head right over there instead of waiting to resolve the issue the next day or next week.

Although network marketing offers many advantages in today's world, it is only as good an opportunity as you make it. If you ignore the increased flexibility and chance to connect with people that it provides, you will have missed the major benefits of pursuing this opportunity.

You also can teach your children to have a balanced life. You can be a football coach or a karate instructor. You can even teach your children how to garden or knit a sweater. You can introduce them to the hobbies and pastimes that make you happy with your life.

Network marketing also teaches the next generation the value of working. Even young children can help out in the business by riding with you to make deliveries or putting brochures into envelopes. But more important, everyone in the family sees that hard work brings results.

In the Consumer Mindset

The marketplace is very cluttered. People have lots of choices to make about what to buy and from whom. Most people will tell you that they have too many choices and are bombarded with too many messages that try to convince them that one product really is better than another.

Just look at the toothpaste aisle in a grocery store. Yes, every product is slightly different. It may be a different color, or have a different taste, or parade some other little distinguishing characteristic. But is there one product that's unarguably the best? Not likely.

This trend began in the postwar production era of the 1950s. For generations who had primarily been raised in rural areas, the sudden access to "stuff" was very exciting. And so large department stores and shopping malls were designed to provide a smorgasbord of products to an eager clientele.

FACTS

As people begin to recognize the value in their close group of family and friends, network marketing is seeing an increase in business. People don't want to buy from impersonal megastores when they can have a pleasant interaction with a friend and meet their needs at the same time.

Today, many consumers are starting to find these large stores more frustrating and confusing than exciting. They want just one thing but have to spend an hour looking for exactly what they need among aisles of nearly identical merchandise.

A Return to Old Shopping Styles

Trends show that more people are turning to old-fashioned methods of purchasing what they need. They are rejecting the mass-market approach and looking for purchasing methods that satisfy their emotional as well as physical needs.

For example, many people are starting to reject the massive amounts of advertising they see, hear, and read. Instead, they are looking to friends, family members, and publications such as the Consumer Reports to make their purchasing decisions. They want to know that a product is good before they buy it themselves.

Likewise, people are looking to buy more from people. It's no surprise that boutiques are replacing the massive department stores in many urban centers. People don't want to be nameless, faceless customers. They want the salesperson to know them and to suggest items that would appeal uniquely to them.

Finally, people are finding that they are just too busy to do their shopping during regular store hours. They like to peruse a catalog at midnight or place an order for merchandise after the children have gone to bed. That's the reason Internet shopping has become so popular. By being able to do it when and where they want, consumers have discovered that shopping is suddenly fun and relaxing again.

Network Marketing Provides It All

Network marketing provides the answers to the new consumer mindset. It is the one and only marketing and sales strategy in existence that meets the changing consumer's every need.

For example, your customers can browse through your Web site or your catalog at their leisure. They can read your brochures in the bathtub or on an airplane. They can browse through it while the kids are outside playing or while they wait for junior's soccer game to end.

In network marketing, you are the "boutique," learning your customer's needs and meeting them as closely as you can. You know your customer as a real person, recognizing when his or her needs might change. You can suggest items for other family members or things that meet their specific needs because of their hobbies.

Most network-marketing companies let their customers order over the Internet, and you have the option of allowing your customers to e-mail you their orders. In addition, your customers know that they can call you anytime, whether in the evenings or on weekends, if they need to ask a question.

Network-marketing companies are generally able to provide more value and quality than a mass merchandiser. Your products may be better made than similar items found in department stores; and they may be made with natural products, providing reassurance to the consumer that they are safe.

In addition, most referrals for new customers come through some sort of personal relationship so the customer feels satisfied that his or her informal "advisors" are happy with the product. You may be that advisor yourself.

The Impact of the Internet

More than any other technology, the Internet is changing the face of network marketing. It allows you to do more and reach farther than you ever could before because it isn't limited by geography. Send a message to rural South Africa and it arrives as quickly as to your next-door neighbor.

Although it started as an academic tool, used so scientific researchers could quickly share information, the Internet is emerging as a formidable business tool. Many organizations post information that can be useful to you, such as member lists and tax forms. You can also find resources such as legal advice and accounting advice because you have unlimited access to consultants who are willing to help you solve business problems.

Perhaps the most exciting part of the Internet is that it is available to everyone. If you don't own a computer, your local library should have at least one Internet-connected computer that you can access daily. You don't need thousands of dollars or any expert knowledge to get a great deal of use out of the Internet.

The Good News for Network Marketing

For network marketers, this is great news. It means you can quickly, easily, and cost-effectively do business activities that would otherwise be impossible:

- You can send out messages to hundreds of customers within minutes.
- Your customers can browse online catalogs of your products and e-mail you orders any time of the day or night.
- You can find new prospects through various online resources.
- You can find new sales and marketing ideas through Web sites and online publications.
- You can easily get in touch with customers and your down-line members no matter how far apart you are.
- You can find new customers and distributors from around the world without ever leaving your desk.
- You can find and research new network-marketing opportunities.

The Problem with the Internet

Unfortunately, the Internet is also a fertile ground for scams. The FTC tries to police it, but new ploys surface every day. These scams can create very real problems for people who want to get rich quickly. Thousands of people lose their life savings because they didn't take the time to thoroughly check out the opportunity. After all, there was so much information presented on the Web site and it was all so sincere, how could it not be a good opportunity?

ALERT

As more and more Internet-based network-marketing scams are exposed, customers may become more wary of legitimate companies. This could affect efforts to recruit new distributors.

Another problem is that every time there is an Internet scam involving multilevel marketing, good network-marketing opportunities receive a little more skepticism. In the near future, you may actually find that it is harder to use the Internet to recruit new distributors because people have become wary of any opportunity that promises them financial freedom.

What's Next: Viral Marketing

Some savvy businesspeople are starting to look at the problems inherent in network marketing and are working to find solutions that meet the needs of more people who want to work for themselves. The most promising result to date is viral marketing.

The idea is to build a network at lightning speed. Instead of people building networks that spread out like a spider web, they find that the interest in the product spreads so fast it's more like a virus. Of course, there have always been get-rich-quick scams that have relied on similar strategies, but in this case, it's a defined, legal marketing strategy that is taking advantage of the changing face of the consumer marketplace.

The Customer Network Marketer

In these situations, prospecting becomes a much larger component of the sales strategy and two distinct networks are created. First is the customer network. Every customer can become a small-scale network marketer if she wants to. She is paid a certain amount of money, often $1 to $2, for every name provided to the product salesperson, as long as the new prospect ends up buying a single product.

Often there is not even a minimum purchase necessary for the customer to receive the commission. In most programs, the bonus will go down to a second level and even third level, giving the customer network marketer even more incentive to provide good names and build a small network of his own.

In addition to the incentive to the customer to provide good names, the people on the customer's list also feel an allegiance to their friend who provided the name, building on the burgeoning need for social elements in the sales contact. People know that their friends are going to make a bit of money if they try the product. They also feel as though the friend has recommended the item so they are more likely to give it a try.

The advantages are obvious. By using this tool to develop a solid prospect list, the product salesperson is freed to concentrate more on sales of the product and the business opportunity.

Future Innovations

The combined trends of a global marketplace and an increasingly restless consumer will likely spur other innovations in network marketing. Already, we have seen it gain legitimacy at the campuses of the nation's best business universities and in the boardrooms of some of the biggest companies.

As business minds continue to see that network marketing offers very real advantages in uncertain marketplaces, they will bring their intellects and talents to bear to refine a system that is already working so well.

Look for even more exciting opportunities in network marketing as we head into the twenty-first century.

APPENDIX A

Additional Resources

There is no shortage of information about network marketing, if you just know where to look. Use these resources to find out everything from how your company is doing internationally to finding new ways to generate sales leads. Keep track of legal issues or find new sales training courses. It's all here!

NETWORK MARKETING AROUND THE WORLD

▨ World Federation of Direct Selling Associations
www.wfdsa.org

The goal of this association is to support direct-selling organizations in the areas of governance, education, communications, consumer protection, and business ethics. It also lists network-marketing companies around the world.

▨ Direct Sales World
www.directsalesworld.com

This organization is devoted to worldwide direct sales. It lists network-marketing opportunities around the world as well as issues and laws affecting specific countries, keeps a running account of which countries offer the best opportunities, and offers books and audiotapes on sales skills and other topics.

▨ Multi-Level Marketing International Association
www.mlmia.com

This association offers a library, educational materials, a chat room, and a place to order books and audio-tapes. It has a code of ethics for direct marketers and also lists multilevel marketing trade shows and conferences. It also provides links to experts in network marketing business and law.

NETWORK MARKETING IN THE UNITED STATES

▨ The Direct Selling Association
www.dsa.org

This association offers many resources for improving network-marketing skills, including books and audio-tapes. It includes articles on specific subjects, such as closing a sale. It also lists members who subscribe to a code of ethics.

▨ mLmSuccess.com
www.mlmsuccess.com

This organization offers a biweekly newsletter that presents direct-sales tips. It has a library, an online forum, and a marketplace for purchasing books and audiotapes. It also lists current network-marketing opportunities and presents news about the industry.

▨ MLM University
www.mlmu.com

This organization sponsors classes and speakers on multilevel marketing. It presents basic sales and marketing tips on the Web site and in a newsletter. It also offers reports, coaching, and audiotapes.

PROTECTING YOUR BUSINESS

▨ Better Business Bureau
www.bbb.org

This 142-member organization keeps a database of all companies consumers have complained about, no matter what the issue and no matter whether the complaint was legitimate or not. It also helps resolve complaints against companies.

▨ Federal Trade Commission
www.ftc.gov

The FTC deals with high-level issues such as business privacy and curtailing monopolies. It watches multi-level marketing organizations closely to ensure they aren't pyramid schemes.

▨ National Association of Attorneys General
www.naag.org

This site lists all fifty state attorneys general and presents information about areas the attorneys general are especially interested in working in. If a multilevel marketing opportunity is unethical, it will likely be listed in their database.

BUSINESS-BUILDING RESOURCES

▨ *Network Marketing Lifestyles* magazine
www.mlmreview.com/nml.html

This publication, which features people and network-marketing companies, gives general tips for success in the business and provides advice from the point of view of people who have made it to the top.

■ MLM.com
✐ *www.mlm.com*

This organization provides articles on multilevel-marketing sales strategies. It looks at new companies and trends in the industry. It also lists products, suppliers, and a calendar of events for the industry.

■ *Money Maker's Monthly* magazine
✐ *www.moneymakersmonthly.com*

This publication presents news about multilevel marketing, resources for finding out about opportunities and sales training, and a frequently updated file of legal issues surrounding network marketing.

■ Jeffrey Babener
✐ *www.mlmlegal.com*

Mr. Babener is an attorney specializing in network marketing. His site offers updates on legal issues in the field, a list of conferences he conducts, and information on retaining his services. He also offers a newsletter, books, and audiotapes on all facets of network marketing.

■ *Entrepreneur* magazine
✐ *www.entrepreneurmag.com*

This publication focuses on small business and frequently profiles network-marketing opportunities and successful network marketers. It also gives good advice for at-home workers on everything from sales and marketing to setting up an office.

■ Small Business Administration
✐ *www.sba.gov*

This site provides information on starting and running a small business.

■ BizOffice.com
✐ *www.bizoffice.com*

This site provides information and resources on running a small business. It offers links to other Web sites that provide business opportunities and research on network marketing.

MARKETING RESOURCES

■ U.S. Census Bureau
✐ *www.census.gov*

This is the public database for all U.S. government census statistics. The site offers general statistics and special reports on trends.

■ U.S. Department of Education
✐ *www.ed.gov*

This site provides statistics on education in the United States broken down into small demographic groups.

■ U.S. Bureau of Labor Statistics
✐ *www.bls.gov*

This site offers all public statistics on the U.S. labor force. It presents trends, reports, and demographic information on every type of worker in every community in the United States.

■ *American Demographics* magazine
✐ *www.demographics.com*

This publication takes the hard math common to demographic information and presents it in a fun, easy-to-understand style. It looks at demographic trends and analyzes them in terms of past trends.

■ American Marketing Association
✐ *www.ama.org*

This association offers research reports focused on marketing trends and information on setting up a marketing plan.

TAX INFORMATION

■ Deloitte & Touche
✐ *www.dtonline.com*

This public accounting firm offers free tax information to individuals and small-business owners. The site also discusses the company's high-end consulting services.

PricewaterhouseCoopers
www.portal.pwcglobal.com

This public accounting firm offers free tax advice through a question-and-answer format. It also discusses legal issues having to do with small businesses.

Intuit
www.intuit.com

This company makes major tax software programs such as Quicken and Turbo Tax. It offers these programs (and others) for sale as well as an online tax center and online tax preparation services.

IRS Online
www.irs.ustreas.gov

This IRS site presents the latest tax laws and advice from the government's perspective. It also provides links to obtaining various tax forms and how to get more information on a specific subject.

FINDING HEALTH INSURANCE

eHealthInsurance.com
www.ehealthinsurance.com

This online insurance broker gives advice on health insurance for small and independent businesses and compares prices of various health insurance options online.

LEAD-GENERATION SERVICES

ProStEP
www.prostepinc.com

This lead-generation service offers prequalified prospects, communication technology, sales and marketing training, and Internet services for generating leads.

Business Network International
www.bni.com

This association is broken into chapters that meet periodically to network. Only one person from each network-marketing organization is allowed in each chapter to ensure that the leads are fresh.

LEADS
www.leadsclub.com

This is a networking organization that puts you in touch with other network marketers to exchange leads and sales ideas.

LeTip International
www.letip.com

This membership organization meets weekly in local groups to exchange leads and sales strategies.

SALES-TRAINING ORGANIZATIONS

Dale Carnegie Training
www.dalecarnegie.com

This company was started more than fifty years ago when Dale Carnegie wanted to help young men jumpstart their sales careers. Today the company offers specific sales programs as well as several Internet forums for asking questions.

Wilson Learning
www.wilsonlearning.com

This organization is known around the world for its sales-training programs. It frequently conducts public seminars aimed at small-business owners.

AchieveGlobal International
www.achieveglobal.com

This training organization offers specific sales training; it prides itself on doing current research to develop programs that meet the needs of a changing marketplace.

APPENDIX B

Network Marketing Forms

The key to success in network marketing is information. The more you know about your prospects, your customers, and your down-line recruits, the better you can sell and motivate. The following sample forms will help you keep track of information that can save you time and make you aware of trends you can use to improve your selling potential.

PROSPECT INFORMATION FORM

Prospect Name: _____

Address: _____

Phone: _____ **E-mail:** _____

How/from whom did I get this name? _____

Has the prospect been introduced to me? _____

Is the prospect familiar with the products I carry? How? _____

_____

What do I know about the prospect's personality? _____

_____

What do I know about the prospect's life? _____

_____

Is this person married? _____ If so, does he or she have children? _____ What are their ages?

_____

Where does this person work? _____

_____

What are this person's hobbies? _____

_____

Contact I have had with the prospect

Date	Type of Contact	Result

Other pertinent information

_____

_____

_____

_____

_____

CUSTOMER INFORMATION FORM

Customer name: _____

Address: _____

Phone: _____ **E-mail:** _____

Date the person first ordered from me: _____

What do I know about this customer's life? _____

_____

Is this person married? _____ If so, does he or she have children? _____ What are their ages?_____

_____

Where does this person work? _____

_____

What are this person's hobbies? _____

_____

How long has s/he lived at this address:_____

Personality style: _____

How did I first meet this person? Date? _____

_____

Order Information

Date   **Products Purchased**

_____

_____

_____

Products the customer frequently buys: _____

Products the customer has been approached to buy but says s/he does not like:_____

Marketing Contacts

Date   **Type of Contact**   **Result**

_____

_____

_____

Prospect for becoming a distributor? _____

DOWN-LINE MEMBER INFORMATION FORM

Name: _____

Date became a distributor: _____

Who is this person's direct sponsor? _____

Address: _____

Home phone: _____   Work phone: _____

Mobile phone: _____   Fax: _____

E-mail: _____   Web site: _____

Approximate age: _____   Hobbies: _____

Full-time job or last job: _____

How I first met this person: _____

Spouse's name: _____   Occupation: _____

Children's names and ages: _____

_____

Children's hobbies, interests, etc.: _____

_____

Monthly sales records

Date	Sales Total

Products this person sells especially well: _____

This person's strengths as a salesperson are: _____

This person's weaknesses as a salesperson are: _____

This person is motivated by: _____

Training events this person has attended

Date	Event

Breakthrough ideas this person has given me: _____

Index

A

Accounting services, 153–54
  bookkeeping vs., 154
  company support on, 16–17, 118
  minimizing, 28
  qualifying, 153–54
  referrals for, 153
  taxes and, 44
Advertising, 177–80
  company-sponsored, 116
  content, 178
  local, 177–78
  magazine, 177–78
  newspaper, 177–78
  overview, 177
  radio, 179
  signage, 179–80
  sources, prospects from, 178–79
  word-of-mouth, 229
Affiliate programs, 19–20
  defined, 19
  network vs., 19–20
  variation on, 20
Affirmations, 163–65
  example, 164
  kudos file, 164–65
  personal file, 165
Amazon.com, 8
Amway, 4, 22, 233
Analytic salesperson, 189
AT&T, 8, 260
Auto insurance, 49
Avon, 4

B

Bargain hunters, 196
Binary plans, 88
Blobs, 106
Bonus plans, 85–86
Bookkeeping
  accounting vs., 154
  assistance, 155
  defined, 154

value of, 154–55
Brand names
  as strength, 62
  as weakness, 63
Brick wall, 160–62
  breaking through, 160–61
  chipping away at, 162
  preparing for, 161
Brochures, 115–16. *See also*
  Marketing materials
Business
  advice, 118
  basics, 13–25
  communication in, 36–37
  friendship and, 98–99
  network vs. conventional,
    14–17, 260
  running a, 28
  starting own, 15–17
  strategies folder, 140
  supplies, 117–18
  See also Quitting business;
    Relationships; Self-
    employment; Tough times
Business cards, 150
Business interruption insurance, 49
Business stationery, 149
Business tools
  business cards, 150
  business stationery, 149
  computer/printer, 149
  Internet access, 150–51
  phone, 148–49
Business types
  affiliate programs, 19–20
  conventional, 14–17
  franchises, 17–18
  home-based, 18
  See also Network marketing

C

Cash flow
  trends, 42
  unpredictability of, 42–43

Categories. *See* Customer
  categories
Challenges. *See* Fear; Tough times
CitiGroup, 8, 260
Coaching, sales, 114–15
Cold calls, 215–16
  follow up, 216
  initial contact, 215–16
Commission. *See* Compensation;
  Compensation plans
Commitment level, 130–31, 166–67
  full-time, 130–31, 133–34
  part-time, 130, 133
  professional attitude and,
    131–32
  start-up speed and, 166–67
Communication
  motivation and, 246
  of new business plan, 132–35
  with sponsors, 104–7
  value of, 36–37
  See also Customer
    communication
Companies, evaluating, 67–80
  compensation, 88–94
  distributor roles, 72
  employee roles, 72
  ethics, 70–71
  final decision, 80
  financial status, 70
  hype, sifting through, 79–80
  information required, 69–73
  management team, 71
  ownership structure, 69–70
  product delivery, 72–73
  prospect list for, 68
  pyramids and, 10–11
  return policy, 72–73
  training and, 111–12
  trend identification, 80
  vision/mission, 71–72
Company failure, 250–51
Company research sources,
  73–79

THE EVERYTHING® HOME-BASED BUSINESS BOOK

By Jack Savage

From Setting Up to Cashing Out
THE EVERYTHING HOME-BASED BUSINESS BOOK
Everything you need to know to start and run a successful home-based business
Jack Savage

Trade paperback, $12.95
1-58062-364-6, 288 pages

Are you tired of long commutes and working for somebody else? Imagine calling the shots in a business you love while working out of your home! With *The Everything® Home-Based Business Book*, your dream of starting and running your own business can become a reality! This step-by-step guide covers everything you need to get started, from choosing a name and getting financing to redesigning your living space, calculating expenses, and keeping effective records. It even has great ideas for marketing, promoting, and selling techniques.

OTHER *EVERYTHING®* BOOKS BY ADAMS MEDIA CORPORATION

Everything® **Dessert Cookbook**
$12.95, 1-55850-717-5

Everything® **Diabetes Cookbook**
$14.95, 1-58062-691-2

Everything® **Dieting Book**
$14.95, 1-58062-663-7

Everything® **Digital Photography Book**
$12.95, 1-58062-574-6

Everything® **Dog Book**
$12.95, 1-58062-144-9

Everything® **Dog Training and Tricks Book**
$14.95, 1-58062-666-1

Everything® **Dreams Book**
$12.95, 1-55850-806-6

Everything® **Etiquette Book**
$12.95, 1-55850-807-4

Everything® **Fairy Tales Book**
$12.95, 1-58062-546-0

Everything® **Family Tree Book**
$12.95, 1-55850-763-9

Everything® **Feng Shui Book**
$14.95, 1-58062-587-8

Everything® **Fly-Fishing Book**
$12.95, 1-58062-148-1

Everything® **Games Book**
$12.95, 1-55850-643-8

Everything® **Get-A-Job Book**
$12.95, 1-58062-223-2

Everything® **Get Out of Debt Book**
$12.95, 1-58062-588-6

Everything® **Get Published Book**
$12.95, 1-58062-315-8

Everything® **Get Ready for Baby Book**
$12.95, 1-55850-844-9

Everything® **Get Rich Book**
$12.95, 1-58062-670-X

Everything® **Ghost Book**
$14.95, 1-58062-533-9

Everything® **Golf Book**
$12.95, 1-55850-814-7

Everything® **Grammar and Style Book**
$12.95, 1-58062-573-8

Everything® **Great Thinkers Book**
$14.95, 1-58062-662-9

Everything® **Travel Guide to
The Disneyland Resort®,
California Adventure®,
Universal Studios®, and
Anaheim**
$14.95, 1-58062-742-0

Everything® **Guide to Las Vegas**
$12.95, 1-58062-438-3

Everything® **Guide to New England**
$14.95, 1-58062-589-4

Everything® **Guide to New York City**
$12.95, 1-58062-314-X

Everything® **Travel Guide to Walt Disney
World®, Universal Studios®, and
Greater Orlando, 3rd Edition**
$14.95, 1-58062-743-9

Everything® **Guide to Washington D.C.**
$12.95, 1-58062-313-1

Everything® **Guide to Writing
Children's Books**
$14.95, 1-58062-785-4

Everything® **Guitar Book**
$14.95, 1-58062-555-X

Everything® **Herbal Remedies Book**
$12.95, 1-58062-331-X

Everything® **Home-Based Business Book**
$12.95, 1-58062-364-6

Everything® **Homebuying Book**
$12.95, 1-58062-074-4

Everything® **Homeselling Book**
$12.95, 1-58062-304-2

Everything® **Horse Book**
$12.95, 1-58062-564-9

Everything® **Hot Careers Book**
$12.95, 1-58062-486-3

Everything® **Hypnosis Book**
$14.95, 1-58062-737-4

Everything® **Internet Book**
$12.95, 1-58062-073-6

Everything® **Investing Book**
$12.95, 1-58062-149-X

Everything® **Jewish Wedding Book**
$12.95, 1-55850-801-5

Everything® **Judaism Book**
$14.95, 1-58062-728-5

Everything® **Job Interview Book**
$12.95, 1-58062-493-6

Everything® **Knitting Book**
$14.95, 1-58062-727-7

Everything® **Lawn Care Book**
$12.95, 1-58062-487-1

Everything® **Leadership Book**
$12.95, 1-58062-513-4

Everything® **Learning French Book**
$12.95, 1-58062-649-1

Everything® **Learning Italian Book**
$14.95, 1-58062-724-2

Everything® **Learning Spanish Book**
$12.95, 1-58062-575-4

Everything® **Low-Carb Cookbook**
$14.95, 1-58062-784-6

Everything® **Low-Fat High-Flavor
Cookbook**
$12.95, 1-55850-802-3

Everything® **Magic Book**
$14.95, 1-58062-418-9

Everything® **Managing People Book**
$12.95, 1-58062-577-0

Everything® **Meditation Book**
$14.95, 1-58062-665-3

Everything® **Menopause Book**
$14.95, 1-58062-741-2

Everything® **Microsoft® Word 2000 Book**
$12.95, 1-58062-306-9

Everything® **Money Book**
$12.95, 1-58062-145-7

Everything® **Mother Goose Book**
$12.95, 1-58062-490-1

Everything® **Motorcycle Book**
$12.95, 1-58062-554-1

Everything® **Mutual Funds Book**
$12.95, 1-58062-419-7

Everything® **Network Marketing Book**
$14.95, 1-58062-736-6

Everything® **Numerology Book**
$14.95, 1-58062-700-5

Everything® **One-Pot Cookbook**
$12.95, 1-58062-186-4

Everything® **Online Business Book**
$12.95, 1-58062-320-4

Everything® **Online Genealogy Book**
$12.95, 1-58062-402-2

Everything® **Online Investing Book**
$12.95, 1-58062-338-7

Everything® **Online Job Search Book**
$12.95, 1-58062-365-4

Everything® **Organize Your Home Book**
$12.95, 1-58062-617-3

Everything® **Pasta Book**
$12.95, 1-55850-719-1

Everything® **Philosophy Book**
$12.95, 1-58062-644-0

Everything® **Pilates Book**
$14.95, 1-58062-738-2

Everything® **Playing Piano and
Keyboards Book**
$12.95, 1-58062-651-3

Everything® **Potty Training Book**
$14.95, 1-58062-740-4

Everything® **Pregnancy Book**
$12.95, 1-58062-146-5

Everything® **Pregnancy Organizer**
$15.00, 1-58062-336-0

Everything® **Project Management Book**
$12.95, 1-58062-583-5

Everything® **Puppy Book**
$12.95, 1-58062-576-2

Everything® **Quick Meals Cookbook**
$14.95, 1-58062-488-X

Everything® **Resume Book**
$12.95, 1-58062-311-5

Everything® **Romance Book**
$12.95, 1-58062-566-5

Everything® **Running Book**
$12.95, 1-58062-618-1

Everything® **Sailing Book, 2nd Ed.**
$12.95, 1-58062-671-8

Everything® **Saints Book**
$12.95, 1-58062-534-7

Everything® **Scrapbooking Book**
$14.95, 1-58062-729-3

Everything® **Selling Book**
$12.95, 1-58062-319-0

Everything® **Shakespeare Book**
$14.95, 1-58062-591-6

Everything® **Slow Cooker Cookbook**
$14.95, 1-58062-667-X

Everything® **Soup Cookbook**
$14.95, 1-58062-556-8

Everything® **Spells and Charms Book**
$12.95, 1-58062-532-0

Everything® **Start Your Own Business Book**
$14.95, 1-58062-650-5

Everything® **Stress Management Book**
$14.95, 1-58062-578-9

Everything® **Study Book**
$12.95, 1-55850-615-2

Everything® **T'ai Chi and QiGong Book**
$12.95, 1-58062-646-7

Everything® **Tall Tales, Legends, and Other Outrageous Lies Book**
$12.95, 1-58062-514-2

Everything® **Tarot Book**
$12.95, 1-58062-191-0

Everything® **Thai Cookbook**
$14.95, 1-58062-733-1

Everything® **Time Management Book**
$12.95, 1-58062-492-8

Everything® **Toasts Book**
$12.95, 1-58062-189-9

Everything® **Toddler Book**
$14.95, 1-58062-592-4

Everything® **Total Fitness Book**
$12.95, 1-58062-318-2

Everything® **Trivia Book**
$12.95, 1-58062-143-0

Everything® **Tropical Fish Book**
$12.95, 1-58062-343-3

Everything® **Vegetarian Cookbook**
$12.95, 1-58062-640-8

Everything® **Vitamins, Minerals, and Nutritional Supplements Book**
$12.95, 1-58062-496-0

Everything® **Weather Book**
$14.95, 1-58062-668-8

Everything® **Wedding Book, 2nd Ed.**
$14.95, 1-58062-190-2

Everything® **Wedding Checklist**
$7.95, 1-58062-456-1

Everything® **Wedding Etiquette Book**
$7.95, 1-58062-454-5

Everything® **Wedding Organizer**
$15.00, 1-55850-828-7

Everything® **Wedding Shower Book**
$7.95, 1-58062-188-0

Everything® **Wedding Vows Book**
$7.95, 1-58062-455-3

Everything® **Weddings on a Budget Book**
$9.95, 1-58062-782-X

Everything® **Weight Training Book**
$12.95, 1-58062-593-2

Everything® **Wicca and Witchcraft Book**
$14.95, 1-58062-725-0

Everything® **Wine Book**
$12.95, 1-55850-808-2

Everything® **World War II Book**
$14.95, 1-58062-572-X

Everything® **World's Religions Book**
$14.95, 1-58062-648-3

Everything® **Yoga Book**
$14.95, 1-58062-594-0

*Prices subject to change without notice.

EVERYTHING KIDS' SERIES!

Everything® **Kids' Baseball Book, 2nd Ed.**
$6.95, 1-58062-688-2

Everything® **Kids' Cookbook**
$6.95, 1-58062-658-0

Everything® **Kids' Joke Book**
$6.95, 1-58062-686-6

Everything® **Kids' Mazes Book**
$6.95, 1-58062-558-4

Everything® **Kids' Money Book**
$6.95, 1-58062-685-8

Everything® **Kids' Monsters Book**
$6.95, 1-58062-657-2

Everything® **Kids' Nature Book**
$6.95, 1-58062-684-X

Everything® **Kids' Puzzle Book**
$6.95, 1-58062-687-4

Everything® **Kids' Science Experiments Book**
$6.95, 1-58062-557-6

Everything® **Kids' Soccer Book**
$6.95, 1-58062-642-4

Everything® **Kids' Travel Activity Book**
$6.95, 1-58062-641-6

Available wherever books are sold!
To order, call 800-872-5627, or visit us at everything.com

Everything® is a registered trademark of Adams Media Corporation.